TUSCANY

AND ITS WINES

TUSCANY

AND ITS WINES

HUGH JOHNSON

PHOTOGRAPHS BY ANDY KATZ

CHRONICLE BOOKS

SAN FRANCISCO

First Chronicle Books LLC paperback edition, published in 2005.

Tuscany and its Wines
An appreciation by Hugh Johnson
Principal photography by Andy Katz

Copyright © 2000 by Duncan Baird Publishers
Text copyright © 2000 by Hugh Johnson
Commissioned maps copyright © 2000 by
    Duncan Baird Publishers

Page 144 constitutes a continuation of the copy-right page.

Library of Congress Cataloging-in-Publication Data available.

ISBN: 0-8118-5123-0

Manufactured in China
Typeset in Perpetua

Conceived, created, and designed by Duncan Baird Publishers.

Commissioned maps: Garry Walton

Cover design: Joanne Lee
Cover photography: Andy Katz

Distributed in Canada by
Raincoast Books
9050 Shaughnessy Street
Vancouver, BC V6P 6E5

10 9 8 7 6 5 4 3 2 1

Chronicle Books LLC
85 Second Street
San Francisco, CA 94105

www.chroniclebooks.com

Contents

Introduction

At the end of the twentieth century Tuscany had become half the world's icon of Arcadia. For millions it epitomizes the pleasures of *villegiatura*: the dreamed-of escape from the city, however historic and adorned by art, to a villa in an idealized countryside … countryside captured in the glowing colours of the Renaissance, but familiar from far further back in our faded memories of the classical world.

Virgilian is a lovely word: Tuscany is Virgilian. The *Georgics* are the poet's specific instructions for attaining and maintaining this idyll of country life, from the dressing of vines to the olive harvest and the proper management of bees. But far beyond Virgil, in the time of legends, we picture the smiling Etruscans tilling the same land, sitting under the same trellised vines, looking out on the same blue receding hills, glowing inwardly with the same oil and wine.

The oil and wine are the foreground of this happy picture, as much now as they were then. The mythology of Tuscany gives them the role of milk and honey in this promised land. If the myth and the reality were often far apart, the endless stream of tourists were usually ready to forgive. As Henry James wrote, "The fond appraiser, the infatuated alien" dotes on a "mellow mouldering surface, some hint of colour, some accident of atmosphere … just because it is Florence, it is Italy."

It is the Tuscan paradox that this cradle of creativity, a culture whose instinctive artistry has inspired the world ever since, has, until recently, been relatively backward when it comes to the arts of the table. Compared with the French genius for exploring the savours of every *terroir*, the Tuscans took their lovely land for granted. For all their intensive cultivation of the landscape, their stately villas and ingenious gardens, even the proudest rulers of Tuscany were with few exceptions happy with simple rations, and rarely seem to

have bothered over much about their wine.

A Florentine feast under the Medici was a spectacle, but scarcely epicurean. "An Italian banquet," said Michel de Montaigne, "would be a light meal in France." Tuscany's foremost chefs to this day repeat as an article of faith that they are wedded to rustic traditions, that they merely refine the *casalinga* classics – farmers' food. And indeed a Tuscan meal is defined by its predictability: bread, oil, beans, roast meat, vegetables, *funghi*, cheese.

To see *crostini*, angular morsels of hard unsalted bread moistened with oil, as an exciting appetizer day after day demands dogged conservatism. The same un-demanding standards have historically applied to Tuscan wine. But the past quarter-century has seen the greatest change in its whole history. The straw-covered Chianti *fiasco* has all but disappeared. Wine has become chic, wine-makers public figures. Tuscany now plays to an international audience. You would not expect her to cut less than a dashing figure.

Times of change are always the most exciting. Over the last generation, Tuscany has turned a peasant culture of suspicion into a fluid and affluent society, translating ideas from round the world into its own inimitable tongue. Tuscany today makes some of the world's most original and resounding red wines, and serves them with deeply satisfying vernacular food. Progress with white wines is slower. The simple seafood wines are there already; adding something finer is top of the agenda.

But does the visitor watching the nodding fishing boats and their rippled reflections from a table on the harbour really care? When the waiter brings you a grilled *bistecca*, maddeningly savoury with salt and oil, are you still indecisive over the wine list – or just revelling in being there, as infatuated as Henry James?

Tuscany and its Wines

Tuscany can be seen, from an imaginary satellite, as a broad triangular basin formed, on its long western side, which stretches almost 150 miles, by the coast of the Tyrrhenian Sea, and to the north, east and south by mountains. Italy's spine, the Apennines, shelters the region from the north, most spectacularly in the Apuan Alps, white marble mountains that from Lucca look snow-covered all year.

The long ridge of mountains continues behind the string of northern cities: Lucca in the west, Pistoia, Prato and Florence. Then the peaks turn south to give the right bank of the Arno a mountainous feel quite different from the left, where the first range of the Chianti hills fills the centre of the basin with a jumble of low peaks and long ridges 40 miles across, rising again towards the coast as the Colline Metallifere, the Hills of Iron.

South of Chianti, the country changes radically into open, rolling pasture punctuated by strange patches of erosion, the *crete*, then rises once more to a wave of hills, each fortress-topped, stretching from Siena to Arezzo. They command the broad Val d'Orcia, dominated to the south by Tuscany's noblest mountain, Monte Amiata, barring the way south to Rome.

The tourists who have poured from all over Europe into Tuscany since the Renaissance have crossed the Apennines either by the coastal route, the Roman Via Aurelia, past the famous marble quarries of Carrara to Lucca, or over the pass from Bologna to Florence.

Today the *autostrada* makes this an uneventful journey; the forests hold no threats. To the walkers and riders of the past the tracks were steep, the forests dense and gloomy, and the thought of wolves and bears a reason to hurry on. Michel de Montaigne, paying his first visit to Tuscany from Bordeaux in 1581, having travelled through Germany and crossed the Alps over the Brenner Pass with ease, described the mountains above Florence

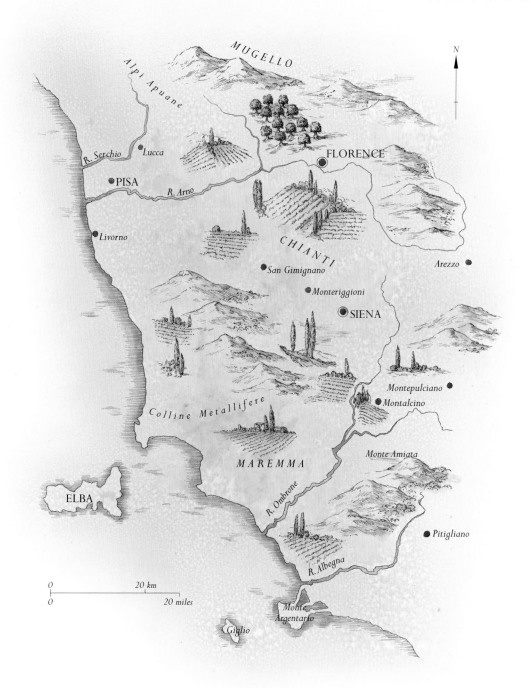

N

MUGELLO

Alpi Apuane

R. Serchio ● *Lucca*

● FLORENCE

● PISA

R. Arno

● *Livorno*

CHIANTI

● *San Gimignano*

● *Arezzo*

● *Monteriggioni*

● SIENA

Colline Metallifere

Montepulciano ●

● *Montalcino*

Monte Amiata

MAREMMA

R. Ombrone

● *Pitigliano*

ELBA

R. Albegna

| 0 | | 20 km |
| 0 | | 20 miles |

Monte Argentario

Giglio

The workforce of contadini *and their oxen in the Tuscan countryside hardly changed in the centuries between the Renaissance and World War II. The mixed cultivation of vines, olives and crops they tended left visitors with a sense of beauty and natural bounty, but left the* contadini *bound in penury to their demanding land.*

as "the most difficult of our journey".

All the more rewarding, then, were the first glimpses into the green valleys of the Mugello, the homeland of the Medici family, and all the more astonishing the spectacularly elaborate gardens of Pratolino, whose grottoes, lakes and fountains were the first evidence of Florentine opulence to greet a 16th-century visitor from the north.

The descent to the Arno valley still presents the spectacle that impressed every visitor of the past: Florence huddled round the soaring dome and gleaming tower of its cathedral, and spread out round Florence, on a score of hills, a concentration of villas and a degree of cultivation unique in Europe. In the 16th century, with 90,000 inhabitants, Florence was more populous than London. Despite the sprawl that has linked it with its neighbouring cities of the plain, Prato and Pistoia, it still presents a picture of serene cultivation cradled among misty surrounding hills.

The passion for *villegiatura* – escape from the city to a villa in the hills – was deep in the psyche of the Medici. They had villas at Careggi (the favourite of Cosimo the Elder) and Castello, both today in the northern outskirts of Florence. There was a Medici villa at Fiesole. Cafaggiolo (also built by Cosimo) and Il Trebbio were their retreats in their native Mugello. The villa of Lorenzo the Magnificent at Poggio a Caiano and the hunting lodge of Artimino lie further west down the Arno where Monte Albano rises from the valley.

Meanwhile, to the east of Florence, the coat of arms of the Albizi family, the Medici's great rivals (until Cosimo outmanoeuvred them), is seen crossed with those of another great banking family, the Frescobaldi, on the families' estates of Nipozzano and Pomino, high in the Rufina hills. Rufina, backed by the deep fir forests of Vallombrosa, is like a balcony that surveys the valley of the Arno flowing west to the sea, more or less densely peopled along its northern rim all the way to Lucca and its estuary at Pisa.

The villas of the ruling class were retreats; they were also agricultural enterprises, *fattorie*, whose produce supported large households in the cities. The cities also supplied the market for surplus wine, grain, meat and oil. The Antinori are one family with records of retailing from their lofty Florentine palace in the 14th century. If there was good wine to be had, it was from lordly estates. Among the first to be mentioned are Nipozzano and Carmignano – Nipozzano of the Albizi and Carmignano in rival Medici country, the Montalban hills that still bear the curious name of Barco Reale. (Barco in this case has nothing to do with a boat, but the walls surrounding the vast Medici hunting park between the rivers Arno and Ombrone.)

From the limited amount we know about 14th-century wine, the majority was white. At the Sunday-to-Tuesday wedding of Lorenzo the Magnificent and his Roman bride, Clarice Orsini, "the food and drink were as modest and simple as befits a marriage." The three hundred barrels of wine emptied into copper coolers were for the main part Trebbiano and Vernaccia – white wines from the two grapes (especially the Trebbiano) most commonly grown.

Michelangelo was to give the Vernaccia of San Gimignano one of the few tasting notes that rings down the years. The almost-universal Trebbiano was, and is, difficult to enthuse about. Montaigne seems as good a reference as any: an honest man, and from Bordeaux at that, who rarely failed to remark on his victuals. Rabelais, a tourist half a century before, seems to have kept his opinion to himself.

"Trebisian," as Montaigne called it, could be "very good". At Lucca it was "strong, ripe and by no means delicate," at Florence "sweet and heady" and gave him a

migraine. Evidently the sought-after quality was sweetness, but it was "*une douceur lâche*", a slack or sloppy kind of sweetness, "*insupportable en cette saison*". In any case, Trebbiano was commonly drunk mixed with water and in "extraordinarily small" glasses – a habit Montaigne contrasts with what he had seen, and evidently enjoyed, in Germany: big glasses of wine downed straight.

Red wine was known as *vermiglio*, a term suggesting much the same as "claret" – something pale red and clear. *Vermiglio tondo* was something, presumably, "rounder" and darker. In Florence the best local wines (white or red) to drink were Carmignano, Rufina or Chianti from the

Filippo Mazzei (above right) of Fonterutoli at Castellina in Chianti, a direct descendant of the Mazzei who first called a wine Chianti, 600 years ago, is a leader among those reinventing Chianti today.

villages just to the south such as Impruneta, or, from further south, wines bought in the market at Greve. They still are.

It was not that Tuscan landowners were without ambition for their farms, or averse to drinking better. As early as the beginning of the 17th century Niccolò Capponi wrote *Modo di fare il vino alla francese*. By the end of that century of improvement

(which also saw the invention of sparkling champagne, of the great white burgundies, of the first "botrytis" wine, Tokay, of château claret, and of port) Tuscany was exporting wine to discerning markets – none more so than London. The British consul at Livorno (Leghorn to the English) dealt in "red Florence", Montepulciano and the sweet Moscadello that was then the speciality of Montalcino. "Florence" was apparently always exported in chests of bottles. At a time when barrels were the standard container for transport, the use of bottles was wildly extravagant. It certainly argues a very special wine. Might it have been from Carmignano or Rufina?

But the days of Medici power were coming to an end in an increasingly impoverished land. Florence's trade was failing; its population shrinking. The last more-or-less active Medici Grand Duke, Cosimo III, a gloomy but gluttonous man, did attempt to regulate and define the zones of production of the best wines: Carmignano, Pomino, Chianti and the upper Arno valley. He was one of the first rulers in Europe to do so. But it was one of the last Medici decrees. For the next century and more

Tuscany was part of the Austrian Empire, with only Napoleon's rude incursions as an interlude.

Austrian rule started by being a blessing. The new Grand Duke François, husband of Empress Maria-Theresa of Austria and father of Marie-Antoinette of France, set about reforming the demoralized dukedom. His successor, Peter Leopold, was a thoroughly conscientious ruler. In the improving spirit of the times a group of landowners and scientists formed themselves into the Accademia dei Georgofili (literally, "friends of the earth"). The Grand Duke accommodated them in the heart of the magnificent Uffizi – the offices of the Medici regime, and now Florence's greatest art gallery.

The Accademia is still situated in the middle of the south side of that great claustrophobic arcaded courtyard leading from the Palazzo Vecchio to the river. The academicians included, and still include, members of every noble Tuscan family. Its library contains Proceedings from 1753 on, recording every initiative to upgrade Tuscan agriculture. There was work to do. They include "The Method of Recognizing all the Most Dangerous Ways in which Wine is Adulterated".

Yet even with all these good intentions, very little happened. Nobody is more conservative than a Tuscan peasant, and it was peasants who worked the land. They had grown their vines up trees for 2,000 years and saw no reason to change. It was, as France's philosopher-scientist Jules Guyot, said, "a liberty, equality and vegetable fraternity that destroyed three-quarters of their vigour and fecundity".

Not until the feudal system of share-cropping, the *mezzadria*, could be dismantled – a move the peasants thought would cost them their land – would Tuscany's vineyards come down from the trees, and its vines be rationally planted, properly pruned, and harvested when the grapes were ripe.

Like every old wine-growing country, Tuscany has its native grapes. Some can be traced back to the Middle Ages, some much further – even to contacts with ancient Greece. Overwhelmingly the most important is the Sangiovese. Its name comes from *sanguis Jovis*, the blood of Jupiter, but its origins are probably far older than the Romans. The Etruscans may well have cultivated it. Sangiovese, like many ancient cultivated plants, has mutated many times, for better or worse, to provide clones with bigger or smaller grapes or bunches of grapes, ripening earlier or later, with more or less abundant crops of better or worse quality. The clone widely grown in Tuscany today is the Sangiovese Grosso – but this too has variants: notably the modestly cropping form selected in Montalcino as "Brunello".

Sangiovese has many virtues. Its wines are aromatic, fairly high in acid, feeling satisfyingly tannic and astringent in your mouth. There is a rustic warmth about the flavour that for some reason reminds me of roast chestnuts – and in maturity they can sweeten, in smell and flavour, to suggest strawberries. Lack of colour and leanness of flavour are the Sangiovese faults. The first is the reason why other Tuscan red varieties, the deep-coloured and less acid Canaiolo, Mammolo and Colorino, became traditional blending partners for Sangiovese.

The white Malvasia, derived from the same Greek grape as the Malmsey of Madeira, is a Tuscan grape by adoption, grown and blended with Sangiovese to soften and fill out a wine that can often be thin and acerbic. But far more common – far too common – is the white Trebbiano. Trebbiano brings little to the party but ease of cultivation and size of crop.

The story of modern Tuscan wine, from the first attempts to define Chianti to the Supertuscan championship of the 21st century, is the story of deciding which vines to plant and how to cultivate them.

Increasingly it brings into play the Cabernets, Merlot and the other French grapes that have become international. It has been surprising to see how Tuscan they seem to become on Tuscan soil; the more so at the comparatively high altitudes of inland Chianti, where the climate is more extreme than in, for example, Bordeaux.

Meanwhile there continues a tradition, not confined to Tuscany but particularly treasured here, of making small quantities of what can become a sort of grape elixir: Vin Santo. Holy wine is the obvious and natural translation – though some give it a (perfectly possible) Greek root. There can hardly be a property growing grapes that ignores the tradition of keeping some (usually Trebbiano, but better Malvasia) to dry in a barn over the winter, waiting for the juice to evaporate and the sugars and flavour to concentrate.

Skilfully made Vin Santo can be a sweet, aromatic wine of extraordinary character – or indeed a dry, strong one with a hint of sherry, if that is what the farmer wants. It remains a farm industry, rarely commercialized on a large scale, but poured with ceremony at the end of a visit, sipped at the end of a meal, and often sucked from dry almond biscuits called *cantucci*. Such thoughtful dunking qualifies it as a *vino de mediazione*.

Those who take their Vin Santo very seriously mature it over five or six years in curious elongated miniature barrels known as *carratelli*, which fit in the roofspace of the house, to be exposed, like the best madeira, to extremes of heat and cold. The house of Avignonesi at Montepulciano makes the very best; Antinori's great oenologist, Tachis, wrote the standard work on the subject.

From the terrace at Fonterutoli the Chianti hills roll away south in the haze to a distant crooked skyline. Shading your eyes from the glare, the horizon becomes clearer, in its centre the stark rectangles of a walled city. High above the walls soars an improbably tall tower: the watch-tower of Siena, the Torre del Mangia. Fonterutoli and its owners, the Mazzei family, have looked out over Siena for six centuries.

The three venerable villages around them, Castellina, Radda and Gaiole, were the Florentine front-line in centuries of wars with Siena. Long before Chianti became the name of a wine, they formed the Lega del Chianti, a place-name going back perhaps to the Etruscans. It was Ser Lapo Mazzei who first named a wine Chianti in a surviving document, written in 1398, to his lifelong friend Francesco di Marco Datini, the celebrated merchant of Prato. The wine was white, the apparent preference of the Middle Ages.

The castle, Siena, the family and its preoccupations, the vines, olives and cypresses on the surrounding slopes, have been fixtures for so long that you expect nothing ever to change. This is the Tuscany we feel we all inherit. And yet almost every aspect of Fonterutoli and a hundred comparable estates has spent the past half-century in upheaval. Even the apparently immutable landscape is almost unrecognizable. As the archaic system of share-cropping, the *mezzadria*, came to an end in the 1960s the lives of the *contadini*, "the people of the land", changed radically, and the landscape they created changed with them.

Today the view from the high places of Chianti is of ridge after ridge, wave upon wave, of rolling, irregular hills, for the most part topped with dense oak woods. The predictable details of their valley slopes, of vine and olive, wall, figtree and cypress copse, corn, oak and stream, are as unimportant in the immense sweep as the spume that flecks the faces of ocean rollers. Chianti contrives to be a small country with an outsize landscape that swallows distance in its purple haze.

Look at a photograph of the view from the terrace at Fonterutoli 40 years ago, black and white and grainy as it is, and only Siena on the horizon looks the same. The foreground hills, thickly wooded with oak and clumps of black cypress now, were bare rock and scrub. The land was far more populous and the *contadini* kept animals. Their browsing suppressed the native trees that now once again give much of Chianti its appearance of a forest with cultivated clearings.

Perhaps no agricultural landscape has ever been so poetically lovely as the *cultura promiscua* of Tuscany just those few decades ago. Mixture was at the heart of it: trees with vines, olives with elms and poplars, cabbages with corn, figs, sunflowers and chickens. And in the vineyards the noble Sangiovese growing alongside a dozen other grapes, indifferently black and white.

The fields were more populous than the silent streets of villages – the black-clad *contadini* planting, cultivating and cropping with hardly a pause. At vintage-time families followed the ox-cart into the fields, a single white beast or a yoked pair pulling a wooden vat on wheels. Wide-based ladders were propped against the trees to reach vines draped in baroque festoons. As the ancient vat filled with grapes, black and white together, their green stalks still attached, the farmer stood beside it with a thick stick, plunging it in like a cudgel to break the bunches and allow room for more. The inky mixture began to ferment in the sunshine, beaded bubbles appearing among the gleam of skins and tangle of stalks.

At breakfast the farmer passed round an old *fiasco*, its straw purple with use, to fill thick tumblers with last year's wine. It was black as night, bitter, sour and sweet at the same time. It washed down hard bread and sweet grapes in handfuls.

It was impossible not to think of Virgil's *Georgics*, the countryman's calendar of two thousand years ago. What

*Chianti at the beginning of the 20th century was not the groomed and fecund landscape we see today. A hunting party at
Badia a Passignano finds its game in goat-torn scrub.*

little change there had been, you felt, was hardly for the better. Virgil's slaves may have been bound to the land, whereas these peasants might have cousins in America. But a share-cropper has the minimum motivation, the narrowest horizons. The Tuscans, wrote Henry James, have "the faculty of making much of common things and converting small occasions into great pleasures". They have been taught by long experience. As Virgil, whose love of the land is as clear in his poem as the spring smell of growing grass, acknowledged, "the dressing of vines is never finished … admire a spacious vineyard if you like, but farm a small one."

If good wine ever came of this primitive way of working, it was by accident or lucky chance. Grapes hanging far from the ground in the trees ripen unevenly – if at all. The many varieties mixed in the vineyard ripened, in any case, at different times, but were all picked together. The vat was only approximately cleaned, sharp with the smell of vinegar. The green stalks, macerating in the juice, imparted bitter tannins. Exposure to the sun while the vat was being filled oxidized the juice, even if a handful of sulphur was chucked in from time to time.

Back at the *cantina*, the press-house, the juice was pumped out into antediluvian barrels before the sons of the house took off their trousers and, hanging on to the edge of the vat, trod the pulp and pips and stalks until it was juicy enough to be bucketed up. Finally the slop was shovelled into the old upright basket-press and squeezed with might and main: the tannins from the stalks might make it bitter, but they could help to preserve a wine that was, at best, doubtfully stable.

Fermentation started merrily enough, filling the air with heady smells, while everyone got out of the *cantina* to avoid suffocation. It rarely proceeded to the end, though, as it should, converting all the sugar to alcohol. The wine remained sweetish, and kept bubbling in a desultory way, even when it was racked from the barrel into another – the one they filled the raffia-covered *fiaschi* from. The sweetness and fizz helped to mask the bitterness and the sharp onset of vinegar.

The best chance to redeem this wine and make it saleable was the *governo*. This process could lift it on to a higher plain of strength and flavour. Some of the best and ripest bunches (especially of Canaiolo) were kept back, sometimes hung in the rafters or laid on straw-covered shelves, to shrivel slightly and concentrate their sugar. Then when the fermentation had almost stopped, popping only an occasional bubble, the *governo* was trodden and added to the chosen barrel. The extra grape sugar could do several things, according to the cellar conditions; above all the cellar temperature. It could kick-start an unfinished fermentation, resulting in stronger and more stable wine. It could provoke a malolactic fermentation that would soften and mellow the green acidity. And it could lead to the pleasing prickle that has traditionally been a trait of young Chianti.

Here or hereabouts is where most of Tuscany was in the 1950s. There was no commercial demand in Italy for anything better. (Those who cared made their own wine.) The famous old names of Montepulciano and Montalcino were virtually in abeyance.

Despite the efforts of a *consorzio* created to protect its good name, most Chianti, even for export, was made to very basic standards, to sell largely to the Italian emigrant population of the Americas. The cheerful *fiasco* of *trattorie* round the world told the story: that with rare exceptions Chianti was thin stuff from a peasant tradition.

Worse, this kind of Chianti was enshrined in law. A commission under Mussolini in the 1930s had taken the name of Chianti from its original home (now called Classico) and given it to most of Tuscany, each province, Grosseto apart, having a "Chianti" of its own.

Desperate, in the 1960s, to bring some order into the genial chaos of Italian wine, the government then legislated to preserve the status quo, however compro-

Florence has been fuelled by Chianti for centuries — most, until the past 20 years, bottled in the round-bottomed flask, or fiasco, *wrapped in raffia to give it protection and a base to stand on. The* fiasco *died because of cost (and the snobbery attached to Bordeaux-style bottles).*

mised. The DOC laws were a valiant attempt to give Italy a system of appellations comparable to the French. But they codified the very formula that had diluted Chianti into insignificance. Specifically, the law called for a proportion of white grapes (up to 30%, with a minimum of 10%) to "soften" the natural asperity of good red Sangiovese and Canaiolo.

The firm of Marchese Antinori, scions of a noble Florentine family, was the first to introduce a Chianti Riserva, a premium wine from their own vineyards blended with others from their friends' farms – with a measure of red Bordeaux to give it international appeal. That was in 1904. But the formula, in the shape of Bordeaux's grape varieties, rather than its wine, would be the road back to success for Tuscany in the 1970s.

Several estates had introduced exotic grapes in the

past for their private interest. The DOC of Carmignano actually called for 10% of Cabernet Sauvignon, based on the practice of its best estate. The cuttings that led to the final triumph of pragmatism came from Bordeaux, too: Cabernet Sauvignon planted in the 1940s on a stony hectare by the sea, remote from any vineyards in an area dedicated to early fruits. It was the whim of Mario Incisa della Rochetta, owner of the rundown San Guido estate near Bolgheri, on the coast south of Livorno. It is much warmer here than in the Chianti hills: vines flower in May and the harvest is in early September.

Incisa's nephews, Lodovico and Piero Antinori, had inherited land there, too. Their young Piemontese wine-maker, Giacomo Tachis, found the San Guido Cabernet excellent. Incisa planted more, until by the 1960s the

The Marquis Piero Antinori (left) and his oenologist, Giacomo Tachis, began the modernization of Tuscan wine in the 1960s and continued to lead it through the 1970s and 1980s. Today a handful of celebrity oenologists are consulted all over Tuscany.

Sassicaia (the name means "stony") vineyard was 57 acres of Cabernet, both Sauvignon and Franc. No DOC for quality red wine existed at Bolgheri. In 1968 Antinori therefore marketed the first Sassicaia as a *vino da tavola*, with no DOC. And while the world woke up to Italy's first unmistakably great Cabernet, Piero Antinori and Tachis were pondering the implications on their Santa Cristina estate in Chianti Classico. From 1969 to 1983 they received regular visits from Bordeaux's most celebrated consultant, Professor Emile Peynaud.

In 1970 Antinori produced a wine under the vineyard name of Tignanello. Technically it was not a Chianti; not a blend but Sangiovese alone, matured in French oak barrels. In 1975 he added Cabernet, and in 1978 launched Solaia, a blend in which the Sangiovese/Cabernet proportions were reversed. These, too, were outside the DOC system, therefore "mere" table wines.

By this time every forward-looking Tuscan proprietor had realized that the old Chianti formula, however Classico, imposed unnecessary limitations on both quality and choice. They let their fancies roam. Merlot looked a promising way of softening acerbic Sangiovese. Syrah might contribute a deeper layer of fruit. French oak added a familiar smell of luxury. The "Supertuscan" was born. And to make the point that this was not a Chianti substitute but something altogether classier, it was bottled in a tall dark heavy bottle, labelled with Florentine flair, and priced where it was bound to be noticed.

That several of the Supertuscans were Italy's most prestigious and expensive wines presented an anomaly, not to say irony, that discredited the whole DOC apparatus. A new category, IGT, was soon created as a portmanteau for aspiring wines with no appropriate DOC. But it was not long before new DOCs were brought into being almost wherever an ambitious producer made a notable but off-piste wine. The process continues.

The Sangiovese is the quintessential Tuscan grape, possibly as ancient as the Etruscans. Many strains or clones have appeared over time, some far too productive, giving thin wine. Its personality is best expressed in forms of Sangiovese Grosso, especially those known as Brunello in Montalcino and Prugnolo Gentile in Montepulciano. In recent years California's wine-growers have seen the virtues of this deliciously astringent grape, too. Its sphere of influence is spreading far beyond its Tuscan home.

The Arno Valley:
Florence to the Sea

The first Tuscan wines to be celebrated and regulated by law came from
the hills around Florence where the city's ruling families had their villas for
hunting, entertaining and growing provisions to supply their palaces in town.

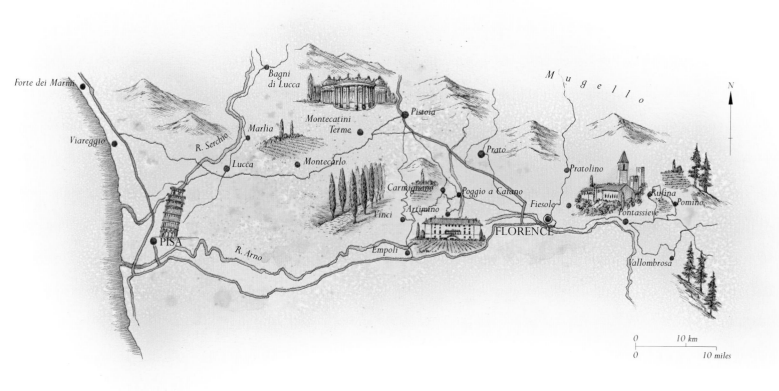

Forte dei Marmi

Viareggio

R. Serchio

Bagni
di Lucca

Marlia

Montecatini
Terme

Pistoia

M u g e l l o

N

Lucca

Montecarlo

Prato

Pratolino

PISA

Vinci

Carmignano

Artimino

Poggio a Caiano

Fiesole

Rufina

Pomino

Pontassieve

FLORENCE

R. Arno

Empoli

Vallombrosa

0   10 km

0   10 miles

The capital of Tuscany is in no sense a wine-town like Bordeaux or Beaune. The city that six hundred years ago reawakened the arts, gave us back classical learning, and can almost be said to have invented modern thought, straddles the Arno with a bridge that seems almost a parody of worldliness – a street of goldsmiths. You are aware of the joy of wealth, the feeling for everyday luxury, in Florence's clothes, its handbags and shoes and innumerable touches of vanity. The markets are rich with every sort of food. Wine seems no big deal. If there are wine warehouses in Florence they are not evident. But in a Florentine *trattoria* the marriage of wine and food is so fundamental that you realize Tuscany can no more run without wine than a truck without diesel.

At the most basic level is the *fiaschetteria*, a bar serving wine and *panini* or simple dishes. At the other, one Florentine establishment has a worldwide reputation for pampering rich wine-lovers. The Enoteca Pinchiorri (illustrated left) is installed in the grander ground-floor rooms, the courtyard and cellars of a *palazzo*. Wine is more temptingly displayed here than anywhere on earth – such a cornucopia of abundance and variety, reaching far beyond Italy, that it is impossible not to be seriously tempted. Waiters may be as professional in France, but here their agile omnipresence is almost feline. The familiar Tuscan insistence on peasant roots for every dish is stretched beyond credence in the midst of such deep napery, such tinkling crystal, such gleaming silver, such a profusion of flowers.

A less extravagant place, and the proper one to pay

continues page 39 ☞

Every distant view of Florence centres on the domes of the Duomo, the Baptistry, and the towers of Giotto's belfry and the Palazzo Vecchio — and leads the eye on to the green surrounding hills.

The Arno in Florence is spanned by a succession of bridges. The Ponte Vecchio was originally lined with butchers' shops, until a Medici Grand Duke decreed that they be replaced by goldsmiths. In the 16th century the Medici built a private gallery running across the bridge from the Uffizi to their new Pitti Palace on the south bank.

The Frescobaldis' ancient Castello di Nipozzano looks out westwards over the wooded hills of Rufina towards Florence and the Arno valley. The red and white wines of Rufina have been held in esteem for 600 years.

homage to Tuscany's greatest man of wine, is the Cantinetta Antinori, installed in the ground floor of the Antinori *palazzo* near the station. What started as a wine snack bar has evolved into a very good country-style restaurant, with the great advantage that the remarkable range of Antinori wines is to hand. For contrast, just round the corner Buca Lapi is a perfect example of the kind of big *trattoria* (*taverna* is the precise term) that has transplanted so triumphantly – especially to the cities of North America.

The tour of Florence's own wine country should start by going up the Arno (follow the Lungarno del Tempio) through Pontassieve, where the river Sieve joins the Arno. Pontassieve is the headquarters of the important wine-house of Ruffino, whose scattered vineyards include some of Chianti's finest. Confusingly, the hills immediately to the north and east are the outlying Chianti zone of Rufina, destined by its steep southern slopes and exceedingly stony soil, sandy but strongly alkaline, to make notably long-lasting Chianti – the best, many think, outside the Classico zone. Indeed, the name Rufina probably loses more than it gains by attachment to Chianti. It was at Pomino, 600 metres up at the edge of the forest, that a French scion of the Albizi family introduced Cabernet, Pinot Noir and Chardonnay to Tuscany. Pomino, which passed by marriage to the Frescobaldi, still makes Tuscany's best-known Chardonnay, Il Benefizio.

It is surprisingly rural, even wild, up here, with the Frescobaldi's Castello di Nipozzano the only visible great estate. (Selvapiana, the *fattoria* just down the hill, also holds its head high.) In this sparsely peopled region the immense view to the south-west, over Florence hidden in wooded hills, cannot have changed significantly in centuries. Still less can have changed in the forest of Vallombrosa, thick with fir and beech, sparkling with

Tuscans are devoted to their funghi *— most famously their plump* porcini, *which are cooked in many ways or eaten raw. The fir forests of Vallombrosa, the Apuan Alps above Lucca and the slopes of Monte Amiata are all good autumn hunting grounds for* funghi.

streams, just to the south. The abbey founded here in the 11th century is now, still deep in the woods, in 17th-century buildings. The solitude and summer freshness made Vallombrosa Florence's fashionable hill-station, where rich families kept villas (Piero Antinori was born here) or stayed in the now-derelict Grand Hotel.

And indeed, going north from Rufina you soon come to the Medici's own green land, the Mugello. At Vicchio they remind you that Fra Angelico was a native, and in tiny Vespignano they will show you Giotto's birthplace. Ponder these things as you arrive back, via the Etruscan citadel of Fiesole with its unmatched overlook, in the capital these country boys adorned.

An even shorter distance west of the city on the Pistoia road takes you to the gentle Monte Albano hills. The cities of Prato and Pistoia continue the urban scene. Each has a *centro storico* well worth visiting, despite their humdrum outskirts and their traffic. Some of Tuscany's

Count Ugo Contini Bonacossi and his family (above) live and work in the Tenuta di Capezzana, a villa built for a Medici daughter at Carmignano in the hills of Monte Albano. Capezzana made the first Tuscan red wine authorized to contain Cabernet Sauvignon.

greatest artists worked in both. Prato, always the textile capital, is said to have more Chinese tailors today than anywhere in Europe. Pistoia has with difficulty lived down its reputation as a city of black feuds. The Germans coined "pistol" from the nasty little dagger carried under every Pistoiese's cloak. Today scores of tree-nurseries take advantage of the alluvial soil in the basin of the river Ombrone – little forests of cedars, cypresses and magnolias.

The old road to Pistoia passes the front of the Medici villa of Poggio a Caiano. The country lane opposite the gates leads directly to the Barco Reale – to the hilltop Villa Artimino (an outstanding restaurant, Da Delfina, provides a terrace to survey its avenues, olive groves and vineyards) and the

vine-clad valleys of Carmignano. Though singled out for honour by its Medici landlords, in the recent past Carmignano's distinction has been its use of Cabernet Sauvignon in its otherwise Chianti-style blend. In the 19th century the Tenuta di Capezzana was one of the many estates of the barons Franchetti, road-builders and postmasters throughout Italy. Raimundo Franchetti married Louise de Rothschild, who reputedly introduced Cabernet cuttings from Château Lafite.

In any case the counts Contini Bonacossi, the owners ever since, maintained Capezzana as a wine apart – distinctive in deep flavour (by Chianti standards) and consistently value for money. Two other *fattorie* that support the tradition are Ambra and Il

continues page 47

Lunch at the Tenuta di Capezzana, prepared in the traditional Tuscan kitchen, is a succession of simple dishes refined by excellent ingredients: home-grown vegetables, home-made pasta, home-caught game and home-pressed oil. Red wines going back to the 1950s are witness to admirable consistency and longevity.

A bottle of Tuscany's best olive oil costs even more than the equivalent wine. The olive harvest follows the grape harvest into winter. Nets are spread under the trees to catch the crop. Lucca's oil is sweet and mild; Chianti's usually more assertive. The best is labelled extra-virgin, but, as with wine, the producer's name is the best guide.

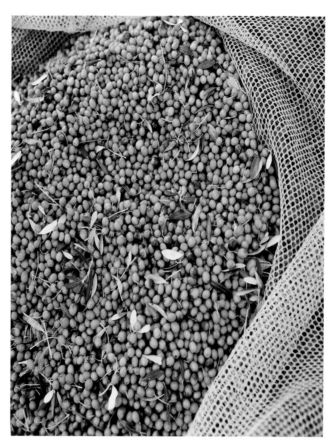

Poggiolo. The area is also technically one of the subzones of Chianti: Chianti Montalbano.

The climate here is mild, at only 200 metres, influenced both by sea breezes coming up the Arno and cool draughts at night from the nearby Apennines. Carmignano faces east towards Florence. Behind the hills, facing west, Leonardo's birthplace of Vinci has an ambitious cooperative *cantina*. (Leonardo's own much-loved vineyard, though, is in Milan.)

From Vinci, the imposing Apuan Alps dominate the skyline to the north-west, their white stony peaks reaching close to 2,000 metres. Their foothills are famously full of healing waters. Montecatini Terme is Italy's most elaborate spa town, with 500 hotels, and the hills west of

it have an air of centuries of comfortable settlement. These Colline Lucchesi stretch west behind Lucca almost to the sea at Viareggio.

Wine is not a major preoccupation here. The one DOC of any renown is Montecarlo, halfway from Montecatini Terme to Lucca, but the vineyards seem as desultory a part of the much-villaed landscape here as elsewhere in these hills. Montecarlo's old reputation is for white wine in which Sauvignon and other aromatic grapes are permitted to pep up the monotony of Trebbiano. Much the best-known producer is Fattoria del Buonamico. Del Teso, Carmignani and Montechiari are others who are experimenting with French varieties. More red wine than white comes from

View towards the Apuan Alps — a range of soaring marble moutains celebrated for their breathtaking scenery and host to the largest cave system in Italy.

Montecarlo today. Cabernet, Merlot and even Syrah are successful. But the whites in the restaurants of Lucca are worth more attention than in most towns of Tuscany.

Indeed, Lucca is a blessed spot. Neither a sprawling city nor a fortress perched on a hill, it sits snug in magnificent ramparts in a fertile valley, its narrow streets, laid out as a Roman camp, largely unchanged in 20 centuries. The two-mile walk round the broad ramparts, shaded by huge plane trees, provides glimpses inwards into the town and its gardens, and outwards to the commanding Alps. Tourists of all times have lingered here, wondering how the feuds, wars and chaos of other cities have failed to abate Lucca's sense of comfort. Luxury indeed: silk made its fortune and, judging by its shops, jewellery continues it.

Tourists in search of cures have left many records of Lucca's hospitality. Montaigne described its wine market, where "every day they bring little flasks of samples to show the foreigners. Very few are good. The whites

The chestnut and beech forests of Vallombrosa are in cool, damp contrast to the hills of Chianti beyond the Arno. The Vallombrosa chestnut trees have long provided sustenance for man (in hard times) and beast (in prosperous ones).

light, sharp and raw, the reds gross." Montecarlo, even then, was the name to look for. To taste Lucca's waters, though, you have to penetrate the hills to the north by winding ways to reach Bagni de Lucca, a tiny spa in a narrow valley threaded by a torrent. Hard to believe that the great names of history have made the journey, even stayed for months. By the 1830s (following Byron's visit) the place was so popular that Europe's first casino – a pretty white building now sadly closed – was built here. Its promoters then moved on to another Monte Carlo.

The wines of Pisa and its region, a few miles to the south, are scarcely rated (except as another fringe Chianti: Colline Pisane). More interesting are the soft Vermentino whites of the coastal flank of the Apuan Alps (their DOC is Candia) around Massa and Carrara and up near the border of Liguria, where the Colli di Luni can produce Vermentino of a soft fragrance that Tuscany is only just beginning to discover and exploit.

South of Florence: Chianti Country

The old road that winds south from Florence's Roman gate up into the hills that overlook Siena is called the Chiantigiana. It opens up a landscape like no other: of castles and villas among vines, olives and cypresses against a background of wild oak woodland. This is Chianti: a country that has never been entirely tamed.

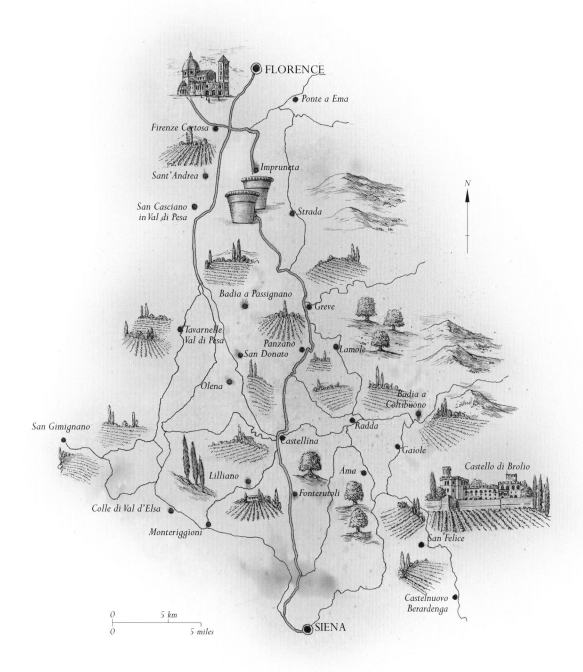

FLORENCE

Ponte a Ema

Firenze Certosa

Imprunata

Sant'Andrea

Strada

San Casciano
in Val di Pesa

N

Badia a Passignano

Greve

Tavarnelle
Val di Pesa

Panzano
San Donato

Lamole

Olena

Badia a
Coltibuono

San Gimignano

Radda

Castellina

Gaiole

Castello di Brolio

Lilliano

Ama

Fonterutoli

Colle di Val d'Elsa

Monteriggioni

San Felice

0   5 km

0   5 miles

Castelnuovo
Berardenga

SIENA

Two ancient roads lead south from Florence. The Via Cassia starts from the Porta Romana, where Henry James walked up through olive groves to a Renaissance villa overlooking the city, and you may do the same. The Torre di Bellosguardo still commands the finest view of all, across the Pitti Palace and the Boboli Gardens, across the Arno and Ponte Vecchio to the tower of the Palazzo Vecchio, Giotto's belfry, the vast red dome of the Duomo and the white one of the baptistry, perfectly lit all day as the sun climbs to the zenith over your right shoulder and falls over your left.

The Via Cassia passes the enormous complex of the Certosa di Galluzzo, the 14th-century Carthusian monastery that commands the approach to the city, before its winding route is superseded by the new Siena road, the Raccordo, a narrow race-track that allows little time for sightseeing.

The Raccordo roughly marks the western flank of the zone of Chianti Classico. In wine terms such villages as Impruneta, just south of Florence (and the great producer of terracotta; a fascinating place to explore) are the southern end of the Colli Fiorentini – the city's daily wine supply through the ages. The first villages going south down the Via Cassia are classified as Colli Fiorentini, too – except for San Casciano in Val di Pesa, where the Villa Antinori stood (it was destroyed in World War II) and where the Antinori still have their principal cellars. Nearby at Sant'Andrea in Percussina the exiled Niccolò Macchiavelli wrote *The Prince*, his treatise on government. His Serristori descendants keep his name alive with Ser Niccolò Cabernet and Il Principe Pinot Noir (he would have had no varietal scruples either). And in Montespertoli the even more ancient family of Guicciardini still make admirable Chianti Colli Fiorentini at their Castello di Poppiano.

The more tempting wine road, though, is the Via

continues page 59

*Pottery is one of the oldest crafts of Florence and its region. The
village of Impruneta is a fascinating place to visit and choose
among thousands of oil jars, lemon pots, and earthenware of all sorts.*

Chiantigiana, which leaves the city heading south-east and snakes south to Siena through the heart of Chianti, the original Chianti zone now distinguished as Chianti Classico. The landscape it crosses is rarely dedicated entirely to vines. That is not the Tuscan way. Untamed oak woods cover most of the innumerable hills and frequently crowd round the road. Olive groves alternate with vineyards in the clearings, increasingly in big pur-poseful plantings marked by tall concrete posts. Desultory tree-growing vines, whose languorous scram-bling up elm and poplar once made the visitor dizzy with

No longer is Tuscany a land where the vine scrambles up the elm. In the 1970s a vast programme of replanting brought the novel sight of regular vine-rows. Much of the new planting was hasty, using poor strains of grapes that encouraged overproduction. Modern planting is more painstaking, and the landscape has absorbed the new rhythm of regularity while losing little of its hypnotic beauty.

beauty, have been banished, along with the patches of iris and corn and cabbage under the olives. Yet Chianti's unmistakable character is still the feeling of settlements in a largely wild landscape. Castle answers castle, villa answers villa and village village from the crests and ridges, where files of black cypress announce habitation.

It is almost impossible to characterize Chianti Classico as it is made today – especially by its best producers. They have long ago thrown out the tired formula that emasculated it with white grapes, making astringency its main feature. Astringent it still is, or should be: Sangiovese grown on heavy limey soil at the high altitudes of Chianti keeps its high acidity and familiar tongue-drying tannins. There are growers who believe deeply in Sangiovese unblended, have planted low-yielding clones and bring them to mouth-filling ripeness. Others add grace-notes of Cabernet or Merlot, and often French oak to please foreign palates. The aged (and

The Renaissance villa of Vignamaggio is one of the finest, earliest and most formal in the remote Chianti
countryside. Monna Lisa Gherardini, known to posterity as the Mona Lisa, was born here in 1479.

expensive) Riservas are the centre of this sort of oeno-logical attention. It is often just as satisfying to choose a simple current vintage from a good house – the sort of warm, lively wine with a gentle rasp, not especially fruity, and not at all oaky, that defines Tuscany at table.

The road-town of Strada is the northern limit of the Classico zone. The road starts climbing here, wooded and wild, to heights where the views are immense, distant villages a misty silhouette, then drops between hilltop castles, Vicchiomaggio to the right, Uzzano to the left, into the valley of the river Greve. On the valley floor, among the files of poplars, sits the little town of Greve in Chianti, in its heart the famous porticoed, funnel-shaped marketplace where the wine-dealers of Renaissance

The porticoed piazza *at Greve in Chianti has for centuries been a market for the wines of Chianti on the road to Florence. The local hero, celebrated by a bronze statue, is the explorer of the Hudson river, Giovanni da Verrazzano, whose name is known to every New Yorker.*

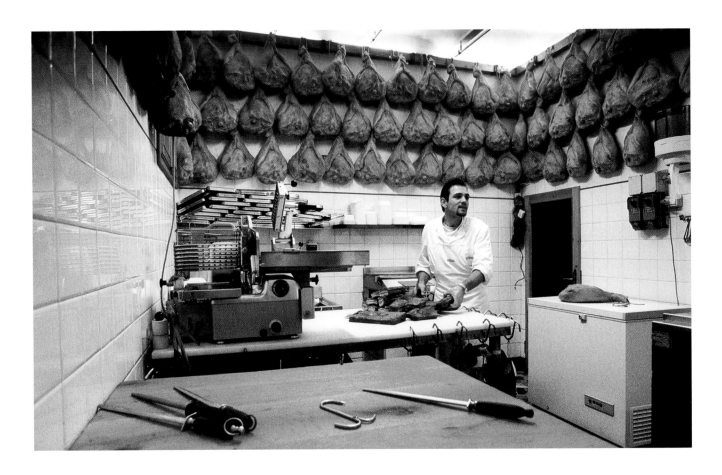

The Falozni family are known far beyond Tuscany for their macelleria *under the portico of Greve, the source of some of Italy's best* prosciutto *and* salumi *(the generic word for sausages).*

Florence came for Chianti from the hinterland. Hidden in the hills to the south lies the stately Renaissance villa of Vignamaggio, where the 14th-century merchant of Prato bought his (white) Chianti – and where the Mona Lisa was born.

The best wines of Greve today – it is a long list – come from the castle estates of Vicchiomaggio and Querceto, Verrazzano (the explorer of the Hudson river has a statue in the Greve marketplace) and Ruggero, and also the *fattorie* of Nozzole (owned by the Ruffino family), La Querciabella, Carpineto, Vecchie Terre di Montefili – and once again Vignamaggio. No particular characteristic links these scattered properties on varied soils, but the climate here is marginally cooler and the soil often lighter than further south. Wines from this northern part of Chianti have in the past been reputed less strong and durable than those from the south, though capable of lovely fragrance, some say of violets, others orris, the root of the florentine iris. Such tentative findings, though, have little meaning in this age of experiment, when many makers are putting at least as much emphasis on their non-traditional wines. Memories of Bordeaux or the Rhône crop up without warning.

To explore the Chianti country in any depth you must turn off the main roads – such as they are – on to the narrow "white roads", the *strade bianche*. Even where they have acquired a coating of tar, the 30 kph speed limit is foolhardy. You wind between dazzling silver olives, into a tunnel of dark cypress and pine, round bends above unfenced cliffs, distracted at every moment by a glimpse of vineyards or the next hill-town framed in a parting of trees, and threatened at every bend by a flying Fiat in the middle of the road.

Narrow roads lead west from Greve to the abbey of Badia a Passignano, as big as a village, high and castellated as a fortress, one of several great abbeys founded by the monks of Vallombrosa. The Antinori family, whose Santa Cristina estate is near by, leased Passignano in the 1980s, when there was still a handful of monks, and restored its vast vathouse and cellars to produce classic Chianti. At Santa Cristina, in the 1970s, the Antinoris made history by departing from the Chianti rules to make the modern Tuscan classics, Tignanello and Solaia.

Following the Chiantigiana south you climb again to another vantage point, the village of Panzano, overlooking a great scoop of valley patchworked with the brown and silver of ploughed olive groves and the green corduroy of vines. Across this valley lie the excellent estates of Fontodi (famous also for Syrah) and the Castello dei Rampolla (where they favour Cabernet). Further west from Panzano towards the Raccordo one of Chianti's most respected and most beautiful estates occupies the two formerly deserted hamlets of Isole and Olena. Here again, Syrah vies with Sangiovese.

A turning left off the Chiantigiana just south of Greve follows the little river up to its source, past Vignamaggio (Mona Lisa's birthplace is inaccessible, but there is a hotel in the grounds) to another of Chianti's historic names, the village of Lamole. If the Lamole wines no longer fetch a premium, the stone-built hamlet, the vines and precipitous woods still make a perfect Chianti cameo. From here the ever whiter and more winding road climbs crazily through oak woods over Monte Querciabella, then down to the rugged hamlet of Volpaia, the highest outpost of the commune of Radda. Castello di Volpaia is the name of the estate, which hides its workings in the houses of a perfect medieval village. With vineyards at 600 metres, its wines are more famous for finesse than fatness. To some, their fragrance and firmness are the nub of Chianti.

Radda is the very heart of the region, with its flanking villages of Castellina to the west and Gaiole to the

Traditional Tuscan barrels are too big to move, destined to store and mature wine for many years. Today the smaller, easily moved Bordeaux barrique *is increasingly seen (and its aromatic French oak tasted) in Tuscan cellars.*

Badia a Passignano is one of the magnificent daughter-houses of the great abbey of Vallombrosa, founded in 1049 in prime Chianti country.
It is now one of the cantine *and a visitor centre of the house of Antinori.*

east. The three formed the Lega del Chianti to defend the Florentine borders from Siena. The greatest concentration of Chianti estates lies just north and south of their lofty positions. Gaiole has perhaps played the leading historical role, as an ancestral home of the Ricasoli family since the 12th century. It was at Brolio that the ascetic Baron Bettino Ricasoli, who was to become the first prime minister of a united Italy (its capital was even briefly at Florence), spent the years of the 1840s perfecting a model for how Chianti should be made.

Ricasoli, at least before he was called to be a statesman, was the most determined of the many landowners who tried to reform their unprofitable estates. He rebuilt the dour brick Sienese-style castle on its 15th-century

stone ramparts and toured France and Germany to study their wines. But rather than importing new varieties his experiments led this proud Tuscan to choose the three best grapes of the region. "Chianti wine," he wrote, "draws most of its bouquet (which is what I aim for) from Sangioveto; from Canaiolo a sweetness that tempers the harshness of the latter … whereas Malvasia … makes it lighter and more suitable for everyday use at table." Sangiovese is indeed astringent, made rounder by Canaiolo (or indeed Cabernet). But his addition of (white) Malvasia for everyday wine was widely used as an excuse for stretching Chianti with the inferior Trebbiano as well.

The names of Ricasoli and Brolio became synonymous with the best Chianti for a century. But it was a sad century for Tuscany: poverty and vine disease led to such an exodus of the *contadini* that the Brolio estate took in three hundred surrounding little farms, their vines neglected and their cottages crumbling.

Brolio today is in the ascendant, Baron Francesco Ricasoli at its head. The region has never seen such prosperity. In Gaiole alone, half a dozen estates are in Chianti's top rank, from the beautiful Vallombrosan abbey in the forest at Badia a Coltibuono (its vineyards are at Monti, the much warmer region south of Gaiole), to the dynamic modern Castello di Ama; and from the little Riecine, founded by an Englishman in 1971 as an act of faith in a depressed industry, to Chianti's one first-class growers' cooperative, known as Chianti Geografico.

Just south of Brolio, Gaiole ends and Castelnuovo Berardenga begins – the south-western corner of the Classico zone, bordering on Siena and the battlefield of Monteaperti, where in 1260 Siena crushed the invading Florentine army. The two outstanding estates of Castelnuovo are Felsina, whose Sangiovese is even more celebrated than its Chianti Classico; and the flowery San Felice, where an entire village has been beautifully restored as both a *cantina* and a summer resort. The landscape here is softer and less challenging, even the roads are perhaps less tortuous than around Radda and Panzano. This is, whatever Florence had to say in the past, the province of Siena, Italy's richest for wine (with the possible exception of Alba and the Langhe hills of Piedmont with their Nebbiolo vines).

Castles and *fattorie* are thick on the ground in the country north of Siena. Castellina is the centre of this zone, another hilltop town (though its chief landmark is a concrete silo), most famous for the historic Mazzei estate of Fonterutoli, flanking the Chiantigiana as you go south, the handsome Castello di Lilliano near by, and the estates of Bibbiano, Castellare, Villa Cerna, Nittardi, Rocca della Macie, San Fabiano … . The leaders of the south-eastern corner of the Classico zone, within sight of the walls of Siena, include some of the most forward-looking producers in all Tuscany.

continues page 78

The castle of Brolio looks south over the parterres on its ramparts and the valley of the Arbia to Siena on the distant skyline. It was a fortress of the Lega del Chianti, the Florentine frontline in the 13th century.

Francesco Ricasoli is responsible for a renaissance in the wines of Brolio, the property of his family for 950 years and the most imposing of Chianti's many castles. It was rebuilt in brick in the 19th century on Italy's first stone bastions, designed by Sangallo four centuries earlier. Time is telescoped by such continuity.

Brolio castle will always be considered the birthplace of modern Chianti. It was in these austere upper rooms that the Baron Bettino Ricasoli lived and worked on his recipe for the region's wine in the 1840s. The gaunt ascetic aristocrat found himself the leader of Tuscany at the Risorgimento and in 1860 became the first prime minister of a united Italy.

And across the Val d'Elsa to the west lies San Gimignano. Is there any reason why here red wine suddenly gives place to white? Because Chianti clay gives place to sandstone? In everything concerned with wine, tradition holds a key role, and San Gimignano had made its yellow Vernaccia time out of mind. Yellow, at least, is what it used to be. The Vernaccia is a local grape only marginally more interesting than Trebbiano. Its historical reputation came from almost sherried wines, of relatively high strength and oxidized in barrels over time – like many Italian whites before the modern fashion for water-pale, bone-dry wines with no trace of fruit and no chance of development.

The craze did hit San Gimignano, and might have resulted in oblivion for Vernaccia, had it not been for the wonderful towered town that provides its brand image.

Badia a Coltibuono is another daughter-house of the abbey of Vallombrosa, secularized by Napoleon and now a private wine estate of seductive charm, with a walled formal garden and magnificent cellars of old vintages.

Inevitably such a medieval survival draws tourists by the thousand. Thirteen of San Gimignano's towers remain out of the 70 that must once have presented a stirring sight. The town walls were built in the 12th century, and the tower-houses shortly afterwards. Why its citizens built upwards, rather than enlarge the city, is not precisely clear. Can there have been so many proud and dangerous rivals, even in those factional times? San Gimignano thrived on the cultivation of the saffron crocus, both as spice and a fine

yellow dye. Indeed, the growing of saffron has recently been revived; you can buy it in the town. The towers are said to have been warehouses for long pieces of precious yellow cloth. But the real-estate conundrum remains.

Vernaccia has moved with the times, too often by being given a taste of new oak, rather than old. Teruzzi e Puthod is a modernizer, Montenidoli a traditionalist, and Prince Strozzi's Fattoria di Cusona makes good examples of both schools. Red wines, though, are gaining ground on white, even in San Gimignano.

San Felice is a whole village that is both a wine-producer of the highest quality and a holiday resort. In place of Tuscan rural austerity its houses and balconies are dressed in flowers and its streets lively with tourists.

The 13 remaining towers of San Gimignano (once there were 70) are among Tuscany's most powerful symbols of ancient conflicts. The white Vernaccia of its vineyards has seen the area's reputation rise again in recent years. Most of its wine-growers, though, are at least equally interested in making red.

The mysterious fortress of Monteriggioni (left) catches the eye of every driver on the Raccordo from Florence to Siena. The mystery is that these formidable walls should contain no more than a humble village, with as many vegetable plots as houses. The reward for the climb from the road is rather a good restaurant.

Siena and the South

Siena links Chianti with another world of wine: wide unwooded uplands
above wheatfields and pasture, sparsely inhabited except for its hilltop
towns. Montalcino and Montepulciano are like independent capitals
surveying the immensity of the Val d'Orcia.

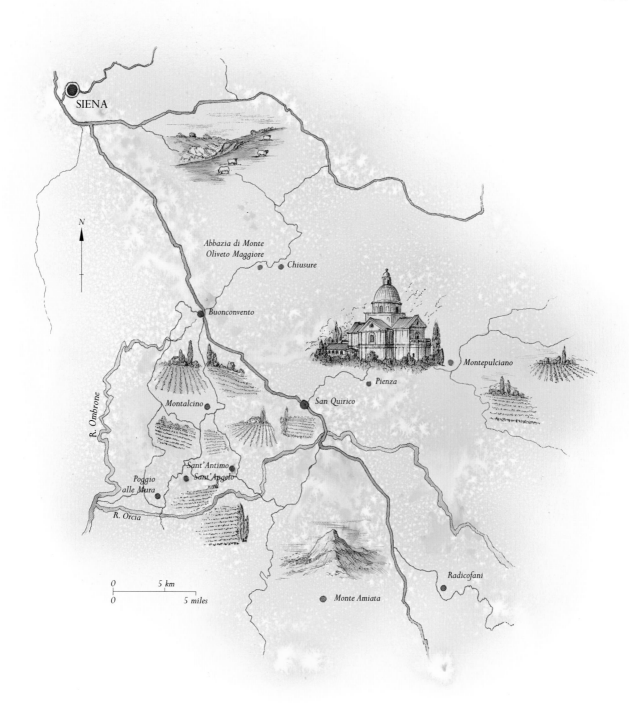

N

SIENA

Abbazia di Monte
Oliveto Maggiore

Chiusure

Buonconvento

Montepulciano

Pienza

R. Ombrone

Montalcino

San Quirico

Sant'Antimo
Sant'Angelo

Poggio
alle Mura

R. Orcia

0   5 km
0   5 miles

Radicofani

Monte Amiata

Is there a more perfect medieval city than Siena left in Europe? Siena formed its character earlier than Florence, built its uncompromising brown-brick buildings in the Gothic spirit, and fell from its height of prosperity before the gaiety of Renaissance architecture could make its mark. The narrow streets between six-storey palaces are utterly unadapted to modern life.

In its early 14th-century heyday Siena was a greater banking city than Florence. Its Monte dei Paschi bank is the oldest in the world (the name conjures up shepherds tending their flocks in the hills; the "Monte", though, were the heaps of gold in the counting-house). In the Palazzo Pubblico the fresco of *Good Government* by Ambrogio Lorenzetti gives a graphic picture of the brief glow of an enlightened republic before the Black Death quartered its population. The Palazzo itself, indeed, in its perfect proportions, with a tower infinitely more graceful than its rival in Florence, seems to symbolize a rare moment of harmony between centuries of mayhem.

It is hard to believe that the glorious scallop-shaped Campo was finished and paved at the same time, nearly 700 years ago – the division of its brick paving into a nine-part fan representing the Council of Nine, the best government the city ever had. A 16th-century visitor recorded that Mass was said daily outside the Palazzo Pubblico while the citizens went about their shopping and gossiping in taverns, with a trumpet to hush them for the moments of solemnity. Today, of course, the Campo is known worldwide for its summer horse races, the *palio*, when scores centuries-old between the *contrade* are brought out, to be put back after the race as unsettled as ever.

Siena is Tuscany's wine capital. Though its sober streets scarcely reflect the fact, its province includes the most productive part of Chianti Classico and the whole of Montalcino and Montepulciano. San Gimignano is its

The Torre del Mangia rises from the Palazzo Pubblico of Siena to overlook the 700-year-old Piazza del Campo and the country for many miles around. It is clearly seen from the hills of Chianti.

source of white wine. All this is celebrated in Siena's mighty Medician fortress of unadorned brick which serves as Italy's most comprehensive *enoteca*.

A tasting of Chiantis under its arches might or might not help you to distinguish between the wines of the seven sub-regions. At one tasting here Chianti Colli Pisane, Pisa's version, was pale and light. A good Colli Senesi was fruity but dry. The Arezzo Chianti, Colli Aretini, was less astringent, with balanced fruit and length. Colli Montalbani was round and sweet with a balsamic note; Colli Fiorentini ripe and warm, chestnutty and astringent; and a mature Chianti Classico flowery-scented, touched with tobacco, a creamy texture giving way to the familiar astringent end. It should go without saying, though, that at least as much depends on the producer and the vintage as on the zone.

South of Siena everything changes. Chianti Colli Senesi may still be the catch-all appellation, but we are in a very different land. Chianti's intricate landscape of farm and forest is left behind. Broad sweeps of pasture and plough take over; wandering flocks of sheep run with jingling bells over a territory of lonely unprotected farms.

To the south-east this landscape suddenly erupts in evil-looking scars and ravines of broken white soil. Montaigne reported "a plain split asunder with horrible crevasses". Surface run-off has eroded the chalk here to form these *crete* as a permanent feature.

The 14th-century abbey of Monte Oliveto Maggiore is a landmark in this open country, black cypresses and pink brick sheltering masterpieces of Sienese painting by Signorelli and Sodoma. And guarding the Via Cassia on its way to Rome crouch the low brick battlements of Buonconvento – again of the 14th century. Not very much seems to have happened in this little agricultural town since the Middle Ages.

Looking south from Buonconvento, though, a ridge

of hills rises to its peak at Montalcino, and dimly behind it rises a distant higher summit: Monte Amiata. Amiata is your constant guide in this region, its summer cloud cap a beacon from Cortona to the coast.

Montalcino is a natural fortress. It was the retreat of the defeated Sienese when their city was taken by the Emperor Charles V. Visitors have compared it to St Emilion – in scale, steepness of streets and shuffle of tiled roofs, at least. Suddenly you are in wine country again, and not only that but wine-boom country, with restaurants and *enoteche* proposing bottles at fabulous prices to an international crowd. In the last years of the 20th century Brunello di Montalcino far outpaced Chianti in esteem; formed, one might say, its own category of Supertuscan.

This southern extension of the Chianti complex has a warmer climate than the true Chianti hills. Vineyards on the steep slopes of Montalcino, which form an approximate pyramid, vary by aspect and altitude. The highest are at 500 metres; their grapes therefore ripen

later. Those on the lower slopes, on the Buonconvento road around Montosoli, and particularly those running southwards to as low as 150 metres in the broad Val d'Orcia, benefit from precocious ripeness in a warm microclimate. It is only 30 miles to the sea and the looming bulk of Monte Amiata is a highly efficient deflector of incoming stormy weather.

The historic avocation of these privileged vineyards was Moscadello, strong sweet muscat that had a reputation even in London in the 18th century, and which remained important into the 20th. Their red wine, made of a clone of Sangiovese known as Brunello, had more body than Chianti, even if the farmers stretched it with white grapes under the Chianti rules. This Sangiovese had all the astringent tannins of its race, but potentially much greater richness, and even more perfume.

While Chianti had its Baron Ricasoli (a reforming wine-producer who later became prime minister of Italy), Montalcino had its champion in Ferruccio Biondi-Santi, a volunteer who marched with Garibaldi, then came home to tend the wine business started by his grandfather, Clemente Santi. At the family estate of Il Greppo, clinging to the east flank of Montalcino at 500 metres, he experimented with his own selected clone of Brunello, pruning the vines very short and picking the grapes very ripe (a nicety little regarded in those days).

By 1880, with the help of his son Tancredi, he had created a completely different wine, robust, aromatic, and above all durable. They stabilized it for five years in big barrels of Slavonian oak, then laid it down in bottle for decades. Nor have the Biondi-Santis ever been over-modest about its qualities; even had they been less so, its price would have kept it in the public eye.

Il Greppo today, approached down a dark avenue of centenarian cypresses, has something of the formal air of one of Bordeaux's grander châteaux. Tancredi's son

continues page 99 ☞

Cypress trees are the drumbeat of the Tuscan landscape, defining its rhythms, quickening its pulse at moments of drama. The avenue leading to the Biondi-Santi estate of Il Greppo is an unmistakable drumroll.

The wine estate of Castello di Argiano overlooks the Val d'Orcia from the southern hills of Montalcino. Below it in the valley lies the ultra-modern winery of Castello Banfi.

Franco is a gentleman of the old school. Talking by the circular pond in the centre of the garden he quietly points out that you are standing on a dead-straight axis formed by four hill-towns: Montalcino, San Quirico d'Orcia, Pienza and, far to the east, Montepulciano. Then he dons a long cape and picks up a cane to take you to his cellars, to see the house's crown jewels and patent of nobility: a few remaining bottles of the 1888 and 1891 vintages. Each time one is opened tasters swear that, frail and lacey as it is, it remains a great wine. Few wine regions on earth have maintained a reputation on such a slender thread of evidence. The Constantia of the Cape is perhaps the only other. But, unlike Constantia, Il Greppo has been made continuously, and the exiguous supply

The brooding shape of Monte Amiata dominates every view over the Val d'Orcia. In summer, thunderstorms often break on its cloudy head, giving its forests a mossy freshness in contrast to the sun-baked valley.

continued to bear out the Biondi-Santis' claims, even when in the 1960s there were only 200 acres of Brunello left in the whole region of Montalcino.

Replanting began in the 1970s. By the end of the 1980s there were nearly 3,100 acres, today nearer 4,000. Two pioneers were neighbours of Il Greppo: the Fattoria dei Barbi and Colle al Matrichese. But when bigger investors moved in they found land easier to buy and conditions more benevolent to the south in the Val d'Orcia, over the legendary smugglers' road known as the *passo di luce spente*, or "pass of the extinguished lights".

Revolution came with the purchase, in the 1970s, of more than 7,000 acres round Sant'Angelo Scalo by Villa Banfi, America's biggest importer of Italian wines. It was an enormous act of faith in their oenologist Ezio Rivella, like Giacomo Tachis a native of Piemonte. Some 2,000 acres of old farmland and scrub were completely

continues page 105 🖘

The new face of Tuscany is epitomized by Castello Banfi, the massive estate created in the 1970s by the Mariani brothers of New York. Their restored castle of Poggio alle Mura towers at the heart of a completely reshaped vineyard landscape.

The Romanesque abbey of Sant'Antimo, long neglected in a quiet valley south of
Montalcino, is once again inhabited today, by monks from Normandy.

reshaped by bulldozers to make rational vineyards. A great California-style winery was built on the valley floor and the medieval castle of Poggio alle Mura, totally restored, was reopened with fanfares and flag-throwing, and renamed Castello Banfi.

In Rivella's masterplan Brunello, surprisingly, was to be a subplot. Rivella was convinced that conditions in the Val d'Orcia were ideal for any grape from Cabernet to Pinot Noir, or Pinot Grigio to Moscadello. He intended to rival Moscato d'Asti with light, sweet fizz for the American market while experimenting with "serious" wines. But red wines soon won: even the long-term goal of large quantities of the rare Brunello.

Other big investors made their mark in the 1970s: Cinzano at Col d'Orcia, also at Sant'Angelo, and the Frescobaldis with Castelgiocondo, a fortress on a ridge

to the west where today their joint venture with Robert Mondavi produces Brunello and Merlot blends under the names of Luce and Lucente. For even the makers of Brunello, a score of them now with names known from San Francisco to Sydney, have become adept at Supertuscan blending. If Cabernet was added to Chianti to enrich a lean brew, Merlot is becoming a natural partner of the burly and tannic Brunello.

The DOC law for Brunello, moreover, insists on two years' barrel-aging and two more in bottle (it used to be four in barrel). Not all are convinced that such long-term investment pays. The answer is to declassify a proportion of the crop into the junior DOC of Rosso di Montalcino, which can be sold after a mere 12 months – a fruitier, easier (and less expensive) wine that many prefer.

The hilltop town of Montalcino has been prosperous before its current boom-time. The Fiaschetteria 1888 (above) has all the bourgeois comforts of the era of crinolines, bowler hats and watch-chains.

The place to review the many labels of modern Montalcino is the *enoteca* in the great grey *fortezza* that sheltered the Sienese. The place to sit and sip a moody Moscadello is the Fiaschetteria 1888 in the narrow main street. How did such a jewel of the *Belle Epoque* – red plush, gilt mirrors and marble tables – come to this lonely citadel before Brunello had been heard of? Clemente Santi's is the memory to toast.

The only road that follows the river Orcia, from the two Sant'Angelos (Scalo and in Colle) with their concentration of Brunello-makers (Banfi, Col d'Orcia, Argiano, Campogiovanni, Il Poggione, Talenti) to the east, is the *strada bianca* to Castelnuovo dell'Abate. It winds through wild country with a magnificent valley view to emerge at one of the loveliest spots in Tuscany: the abbey of Sant'Antimo.

Whether or not it was Charlemagne who founded this abbey, and despite the fact that for five centuries it served no religious purpose, the serene Romanesque interior of Sant'Antimo is an unmistakably sacred space, filled with light that seems to penetrate the very walls and pillars. Happily it has been resettled by French monks, whose Gregorian chant morning and evening hallows the quiet valley of pasture and olives.

With no road up the valley, the choice here is either to go back to Montalcino or to cross the Orcia towards Monte Amiata (even to drive up into the cool of dense beech and chestnut woods) and then double back past the fortress of Rocca d'Orcia to meet the Via Cassia, once again heading for San Quirico. Near where the Cassia crosses the river, the village of Bagno Vignoni has hot springs given an architectural setting by the Medici. In Tuscany you are never far from a leak in the underworld.

In San Quirico a turning east on rising ground takes you to Pienza, the little model city created by a man considered the jewel of his time, Aeneas Silvius Piccolomini.

Halfway up the hill to the lovely walled town of Montepulciano stands the sublime masterpiece of Antonio da Sangallo, the church of San Biagio, consecrated by a Medici pope in 1529. It is an architectural sonata, a temple you cannot tire of.

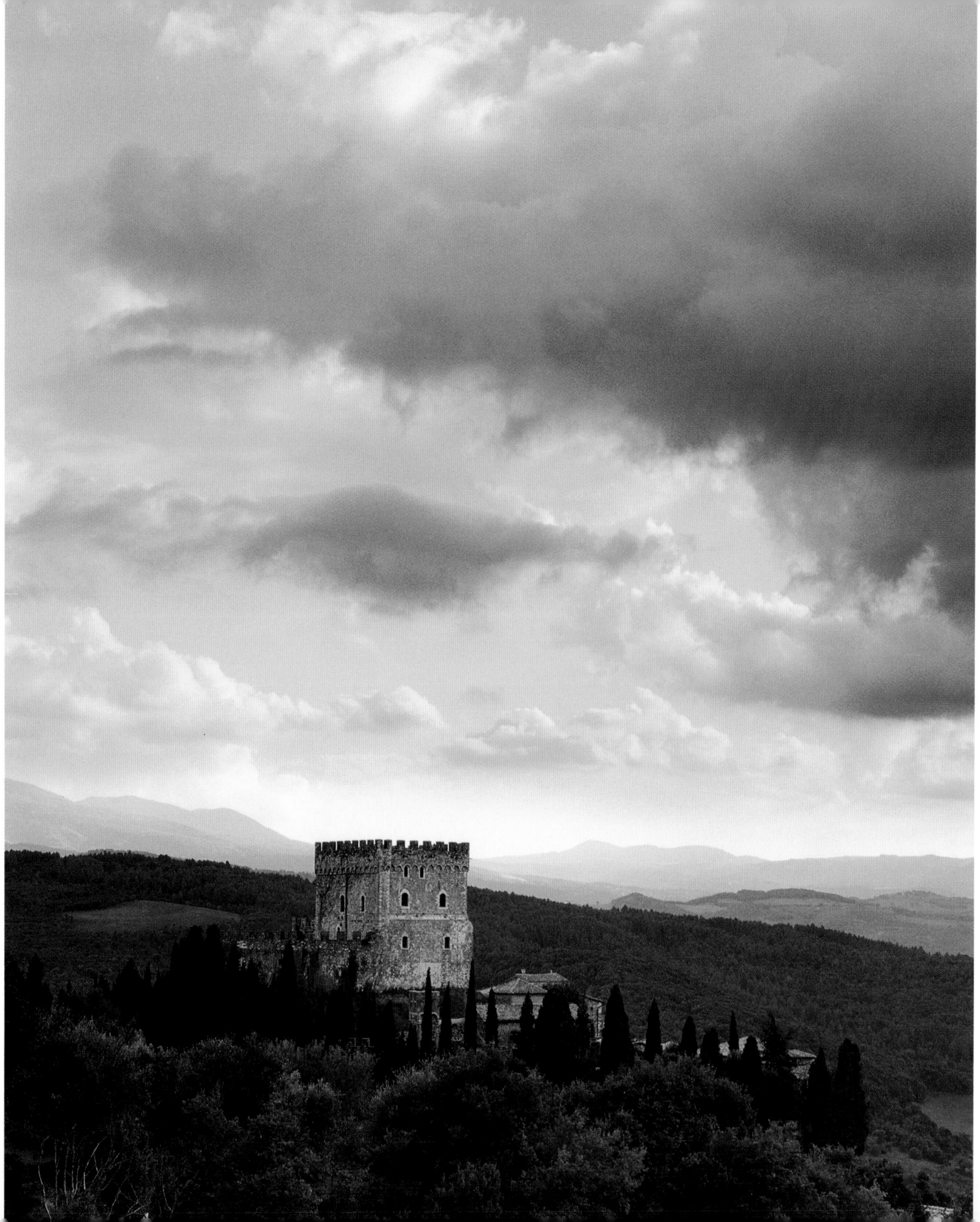

Piccolomini was the complete Renaissance man: diplomat (he visited Scotland for the Pope, finding it extremely uncomfortable, and was seized as a spy in London), scholar in many languages, friend and patron of artists, the most respected figure in Siena, and finally Pope as Pius II. As Pope he rebuilt his native village with an understated unity of composition that amounts to genius. His own palace, by the Duomo, is the perfect Renaissance house, its garden side a three-storey *loggia* of surpassing grace surveying the Val d'Orcia over the town walls.

Besides Monte Amiata, the most striking object in its distant view is Radicofani, a citadel reaching for the sky from a high rock, the next stopping place on the road to Rome. The Medici built the fine stone coaching inn recalled in the memoirs of travellers from Diderot to Horace Walpole and Casanova as damp, draughty and verminous, with dishonest servants and poisonous food. Dickens called it a "forecourt to hell". The inn is no more, but the fortress has become a fascinating museum of its own history from Etruscan times to World War II.

The Val d'Orcia is a place of dramatic skies. Summer storms perch on Amiata, or race east towards the Apennines as black backdrops to villages gilded by the sun. Montepulciano is the last hilltop before the broad Val di Chiana with its *autostrada*. It was once a town of high strategic importance, and is still stately behind its walls. The approach from the Pienza road is heart-stopping, for there, at the foot of the town's high hill, is a perfect Renaissance church seemingly left at random in the fields, its honey-coloured dome and belfry rising from silver olive and black cypress.

Wild, wooded hills alternate with vineyards and olives on the road from Montalcino to Montepulciano, passing through San Quirico and the perfect Renaissance miniature of Pienza with its Palazzo Piccolomini (above).

The wine of Montepulciano is blessed with the peculiar appellation of Vino Nobile. Nobody seems certain why. The name is not very ancient, nor has it often been accurate. Early records show the town making the sweet red Aleatico that is now almost confined to Elba. In days when sweet wines were favourite there would have been some logic in the name. Twentieth-century Vino Nobile, though, was similar in formulation to Chianti (we are still in the Colli Senesi zone) but with a local clone of Sangiovese known as Prugnolo Gentile – whose main character seems to be youthful hardness.

Serious work on justifying the appellation began in the 1970s with the house of Avignonesi, based in a little *palazzo* where some of Tuscany's most sublime Vin Santo – delicate, smoky, orange-perfumed – is aged under the rooftiles. Contucci (in another *palazzo* in town) and Fanetti were older producers of note. They have since been joined by Poliziano (named for the town's

continues page 114

Renaissance poet), Boscarelli, Trerose, Fassati, and recently Antinori and Ruffino, on what is steadily becoming a faster track as Chianti-style additives are eliminated, the Prugnolo tamed, and of course Cabernet and Merlot brought into play. Whether Vino Nobile will ever acquire the cachet of Brunello di Montalcino is doubtful, but the best are serious red wines to keep for several years. Perhaps more likely, in the long run, it will be swamped by exotic Supertuscans.

Montepulciano's vineyards lie on the eastern slopes down to the Chiana and the western slopes beyond the river. The climate is relatively warm and the soil lighter than in Chianti and Montalcino – factors that encourage trials with other grapes, especially Bordeaux varieties, and, more surprisingly, white ones. Bianco Vergine Valdichiana is the prettily named DOC for a strictly bland white. Avignonesi, however, make much more interesting whites of Chardonnay and Sauvignon Blanc

South of Siena sudden eruptions in peaceful, undulating pasture, the limestone scars known as the crete, *look like the result of some violent subterranean struggle.*

(and, moreover, stray outside the DOC area into the next province, Cortona).

Meanwhile, down in the wild Val d'Orcia near Sarteano, and far from any traditional vineyards, one of the least inhibited of all Supertuscan producers, the Tenuta di Trinoro, is making sumptuous reds with an almost Napa touch. A Val d'Orcia DOC has even been created in its honour.

It was not far from here, in a simple restaurant overlooking the Val d'Orcia from the Monte Amiata side, a place so simple there was no written menu, that I encountered Tuscan cooking at its most sublime. The meal started with the pure-tasting *zuppa di verdura*, coiling a green-gold filament of olive oil on the surface. Far from being filling, this soup just prepares you for the "*tre*" of pasta: not three but four different pasta dishes, brought individually and in sequence in big white bowls to the table. First, *tortelli* filled with spinach and sheep's-milk *ricotta*; next, *ravioli* of wild mushrooms; then *pappardelle* with baby artichokes; and finally a *lasagne* filled with seriously meaty sauce. Each was brought to the table by a daughter of the house in friendly simplicity, as though hospitality demanded no less.

There was no white wine even available, but the place is near enough to Montepulciano for the house red in the earthenware jugs to be crisp young rosso, fruity and fighting, giving the palate a brisk rubdown, and deceivingly unheady.

The porker that nourished the huge milk-white chop had clearly never done a day's work: it melted between palate and tongue. And then there was *panna cotta*, Vin Santo, hot, strong, bazaar-scented coffee, *grappa* … . They pretend this is peasant food, your modern Tuscans.

The Tuscan Coast
and the Maremma

Last and, strangely, most remote of Tuscany's wine regions comes
the coast. There is no noble tradition here; but, scattered along the
seaside and back into the Etruscan-haunted heartland, the soil has
begun to yield revolutionary wines. This is Tuscany's New World.

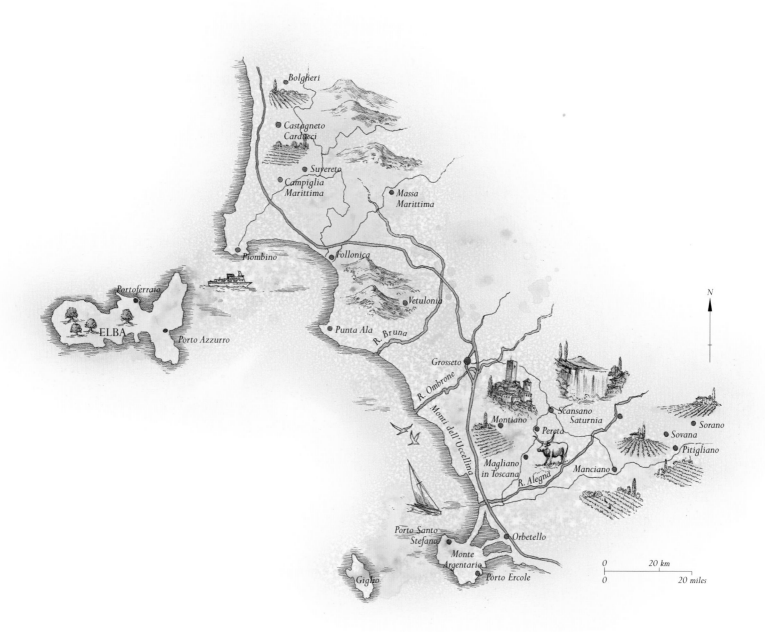

Bolgheri

Castagneto
Carducci

Suvereto

Campiglia
Marittima

Massa
Marittima

Piombino

Follonica

Portoferraio

Vetulonia

ELBA

Porto Azzurro

Punta Ala

R. Bruna

N

Grosseto

R. Ombrone

Montiano

Scansano
Saturnia

Sorano

Monti dell'Uccellina

Pereta

Sovana

Pitigliano

Magliano
in Toscana

Manciano

R. Alegna

Porto Santo
Stefano

Orbetello

Monte
Argentario

Porto Ercole

Giglio

0   20 km

0   20 miles

A tour of Tuscany and its wines in the past, even the recent past, would have had almost nothing to say about the coast. In Etruscan times the coastal plains, the iron mines of the Colline Metallifere and the fertile south were among the busiest parts of Etruria, from Tarquinia (over the border in Lazio) to the three ports of Talamone, Piombino (the Etruscan Populonia), and Pisa to Fiesole. The Romans followed suit. But in the long interim most of the coast became too dangerous to inhabit. Malaria and Moorish marauders were scourges over centuries. In the early 17th century it was still not safe to go fishing from Pisa: African slave-traders raided the beaches. The southern Maremma was garrisoned by the Spanish, who left their star-shaped hill-forts from the Argentario peninsula to Elba.

The villa-based economy that produced wine scarcely existed in this sparsely inhabited region. South and inland, the hill-town of Pitigliano, with a strong Jewish culture, was known for a better white wine than most. Indeed, most of the wine hereabouts was white, or rather *giallo*, the unfortunate jaundiced result of mishandling white grapes. The few who grew Sangiovese knew it by the name of Morellino – and swore that it was aboriginal in the Maremma. Who was to say what other possibilities existed, until the owner of one of the rare coastal estates started dabbling on the property he had bought principally to raise horses? The place was Bolgheri, the estate San Guido, the grapes Cabernet, the vineyard Sassicaia.

Bolgheri is still not easy to find on the map. It is a walled village just inland from the Via Aurelia, the Roman coast road, about midway between the ports of Livorno and Piombino. The coast here is unexciting and relatively inaccessible, without the broad sand beaches that draw crowds further north, or the natural beauty of the gulf of Baratti or the Monti dell'Uccellina further south. In the Middle Ages this was the fief of the della

Tuscany's most famous single vineyard, Sassicaia, lies on low hills overlooking the sea near Bolgheri; land that not long ago grew fruit trees and early crops for market. Its wonderful aptitude for Cabernet Sauvignon was unknown.

Gherardesca family, whose castles dot the region. In the 19th century the poet Carducci brought Bolgheri a measure of fame. But no one would have heard of it today without the initiative of the Marquis Incisa della Rochetta and his plantation of Cabernet in a maritime climate (think of the Médoc) and on the gravelly (think of Graves) outwash of streams draining the Colline Metallifere behind.

His nephews were the brothers Lodovico and Piero Antinori. They joined in: Lodovico on his estate of Ornellaia, at first with Sauvignon Blanc to make a lovely wine called Poggio alle Gazze; then with Cabernet on the gravel and Merlot on a plot of clay called Masseto. Piero started with a rosato called Scalabrone (rosato was formerly the only authorized Bolgheri wine), then chose higher, stony ground for Cabernet and Merlot to make Guado al Tasso. All these names now spell money.

Bolgheri is proving itself to be Tuscany's Bordeaux: planting has now reached 640 acres, with a good dozen proprietors, and reached as far as Castagneto Carducci (named in honour of the poet) six miles to the south, where Angelo Gaja, the irrepressible genius of Barbaresco, has recently put down roots, alongside the well-established estate of Grattamacco.

Enough time has passed for early Sassicaias to have reached full maturity. In 1998 the 1975 vintage was compared in London with the Bordeaux First Growths of this (in Bordeaux) very tannic year. The Sassicaia was the fruitier wine, with a taste of extreme ripeness rarely found in Bordeaux. But it was among its peers.

So far the Bolgheri vineyards are alone in their class.

Cypress trees line up like shuffling pilgrims in the immense avenue leading from the coast road, the ancient Via Aurelia, to the medieval fortified village of Bolgheri.

Which is not to say that experiments are not happening elsewhere on the coast. Just to the north, where the river Cecina flows down from Volterra, Montescudaio is a minor DOC with a respectable performance. At Suvereto, behind Piombino in the hills, Val di Cornia is another DOC to watch. But for all the opportunities offered by coastal conditions this has not yet proved itself serious wine country.

The island of Elba is a case apart. Though its principal calling from Etruscan times has been mining (the massive iron mines only fell silent in the past century), its strong red mineral soil and balmy climate undoubtedly give it the potential to make original wines. Elba's quarter of an hour of fame was as Napoleon's place of exile. The frustrated emperor achieved more in his nine months there than all the island's other rulers combined.

The little capital, Portoferraio, in its beautiful sheltered bay, richly forested since agriculture has dwindled, was fortified by the Medici Grand Dukes, but it is Napoleon's ghost that dominates.

His conversion of the hilltop house with the best views into a toy-town palace is a moving monument. So is the country house where he took his long baths at weekends. He surveyed every square inch of the island, improving everything from roads to sewers. When he stopped to picnic, instead of regretting his Chambertin he swigged Aleatico.

Sweet red muscat is not everybody's first choice. But a good Aleatico (they are rare) is one of the world's true originals – deep red, sometimes with prickling bubbles, muscat-scented, deliciously sweet, insidiously strong and at the same time bracingly tannic. It makes a country

Tuscany has a dozen off-shore islands reached by ferry from Porto Santo Stefano or Piombino. Rocky little Giglio alone specializes in growing a white grape from Sicily (Ansonica) to make its tasty yellow fish-wine.

ham *panino* a Napoleonic experience.

Procanico is Elba's version of Trebbiano, and routinely as dull as that sounds. The white to look for is Ansonica, made from a much tastier Sicilian grape, and the speciality of the tiny island of Giglio. On Elba, Acquabona is the name of the most considerable producer, but the little estate of La Chiusa, on the water's edge opposite Portoferraio, is the one to visit.

The mainland from Elba southwards had a dismal reputation. Dante referred to it as hell on earth. Much of the province of Grosseto was unhealthily marshy, despite repeated attempts at drainage, until Mussolini's time, its inhabitants a mass of wildlife and a few cowboys tending longhorn herds. The wildlife is now largely confined to the conservation area of the Monti dell'Uccellina. Modish resorts at Punta Ala and on the Argentario peninsula bring Milanese and Romans to play. The fertile hills inland, though, are the new frontier for Tuscan wine. News arrives weekly of another prestigious investment as the great names of Chianti, frustrated from expansion nearer home or scenting an exciting alternative, move south into Morellino territory.

This is some of Tuscany's lushest and most peaceful country. Farms are few. The little walled towns of Magliano (known for its millennial olive trees), Capalbio, Pereta and Manciano, with gates and towers, rise undramatically in softly swelling hills. Scansano, self-chosen as the Morellino capital, overlooking them all from 500 metres, has a tremendous view out over dark oaks to the silver Tyrrhenian Sea, the Argentario peninsula, the nearby islands and even

Elba's capital of Portoferraio looks across its deep, sheltered bay to the diminutive walled vineyards of La Chiusa. Red and white wines from here are much as they must have been in Napoleon's time, with fragrant red Aleatico the star.

to the snowcaps of Corsica, hulldown on the horizon.

Other Morellino villages could have had the privilege of becoming the nominal wine capital. The mêlée in the Scansano market is more about horses than wine, with cowboys posing at the bar in leather chaps and the Maremma Stetson. The first people to call their wine Morellino were the Mantellasi family at Magliano early in the last century. Then in 1975 a big new cooperative appropriated it to give Scansano a DOC. Until recently it has been hard to characterize the wine Morellino makes. It is a Sangiovese with good colour, not a Chianti-style blend, with warm body but usually (as made by most of the few producers) lacking much grip or typically Tuscan astringence. Such producers as Banti in Scansano and the respected Moris Farms near Grosseto put up a deluxe version, sadly spoiled by the flavour of new oak — and the crazy price that goes with it. The picture is now emerging, though, of a red of generous character, perhaps even a low-key, easy-going Brunello. Certainly the names of Frescobaldi, Mazzei and even Biondi-Santi on labels (all three, and Antinori, too, have bought land in the district) are giving it a high-profile launch. There is little chance that they will stick to Morellino unblended, however good it could become. All the indications are towards another breed of Supertuscan blends.

Inland, the country immediately south of Monte Amiata has spectacularly emphatic geology. At Saturnia steaming hot springs form a waterfall visible for miles. The Etruscan citadel of Pitigliano stands on an impregnable rock embellished as a stronghold by the Aldobrandeschi, its medieval lords, and their successors, the Counts Orsini of Rome (and of *Twelfth Night*). The 15th-century exodus of Jews from Spain enriched Pitigliano and almost certainly gave its white wine its more than local reputation. At one time it was Tuscany's best known. In this warm region of multi-coloured, purple and orange

The old chaotic mixed cultivation around Pitigliano is giving way to purposeful plantings of a wide range of non-traditional grapes. Sangiovese has a place, but alongside grapes from other parts of Italy, Bordeaux and the Rhône.

Pereta is typical of the walled villages of the Maremma hills around Scansano. Its watch-tower recalls the time when raiders from North Africa
roamed the country looking for potential slaves.

mineral-rich soils, though, there is no reason why white grapes should be better than red. The future is clearly indicated by the recent arrival of the Antinoris, planting both Tuscan and French red grapes (happily, even Aleatico) in the fertile fields around Sovana, a village still haunted by the Etruscans.

Sovana and Sorano are neighbouring villages where little has happened to overlay the Etruscan past. They can still be approached by hidden lanes, sunk as deep as 30 metres into the rock by the Etruscans and lined with their noble architectural tombs, sculpted into the cliff-face. Everything is ancient – how ancient, nobody seems to mind. Sovana's finest Etruscan tomb is known as the Tomba Ildebranda. The village was birthplace to the 11th-century Pope Gregory VII, born Ildebrando. Naturally such an important monument must be his. In the little church is a carved stone shrine and canopy of the ninth century – almost halfway back in time to the Etruscan founders of the village.

Having seen their mischievous smiles (an Etruscan face is unmistakable: their tomb-portraits show them elfin, friendly, faintly mocking) you cannot banish them from your mind. It is a question I love to ponder, how much we share with the ancient inhabitants of Tuscany, or any land. Time stands still in each hidden fold of the enchanted landscape. Life speeds on. What the French call the *terroir*, the essence of place, surely alters very little. Geology underlies it; geography moulds it. All that changes of climate, that poverty or prosperity or changing customs can do will one day be undone, just as the goats leave the land and let its flowers and trees return.

Wine is one of the great carriers of a sense of place and time. Though it is perfectly possible to make it technically neutral, to eliminate all the clues about its background, it is difficult, and certainly pointless. The Australians discovered they could make perfect anonymous wine, and straight away realized that it was

continues page 133

The Etruscan citadels of Sovana and Sorano can be approached by
strange sunken ways dug out of the rock 2,500 years ago. Some lead
to the cliff-faces where the Etruscans carved their monumental
tombs. At Magliano the olive trees are said to be almost as old.

one-glass stuff. As soon as it spoke with an accent again the public was enchanted.

Tuscan wine speaks with an accent. Several accents, to those who can tell a Chianti Classico from a Vino Nobile, or a Morellino from a Carmignano. But is what they are saying specifically Tuscan, or might it be reproduced any-where by treating the same grapes in the same way?

While the Sangiovese remains king its elusive flavour and highly strung texture will mark out Tuscan reds. The tension is between fruit, acidity and tannin with a dis-tinctive patois. Some tannins can be felt as the spinal col-umn of a wine; some as its *charpente* (the word the French use for the supporting structure of a roof). The tannins of Sangiovese coat the whole mouth with a more or less marked astringency. It seasons food and creates thirst at the same time. Too much becomes bitter; the right amount is invigorating, like a rough towel.

Most of today's new trials, aspiring Supertuscans, are

The town of Pitigliano has the most formidable site of any in Tuscany: a great flat-topped rock, sheer on three sides. Etruscan cellars under the fortress-gate sell its sharp white wine.

blends of Sangiovese with imported grapes. The implied intention is to profit from juicier or more aromatic flavours than Sangiovese provides, to flesh out any leanness, but to keep the Sangiovese signature, its sense of the earth, its astringent voice.

But the signature is, of course, more than that of a grape. Plant a Bordeaux grape in the Chianti hills and no one will ever take its wine for Bordeaux. Plant Chardonnay in Rufina and it gives a Florentine wine. The time-hallowed Tuscan varieties certainly express the region most clearly, but it seems that any grape you grow here somehow catches Tuscan habits – however hard they are to pin down in words.

And the most endearing habit they catch is to fall in with the Tuscan feast. Food and wine belong in that order in the Tuscan – in any Italian – mind. Put too much stress on wine and you upset the balance. It is simply bad manners for a wine to assert itself too strongly.

Yet you can stand too close to wine. Watching the chef does not help you enjoy his cooking, and the modern tendency to look over the wine-maker's shoulder may distort as much as it reveals. For wine is many things: food and drink, medicine and status symbol, inspiration and inebriant. Those who really love it, though, want it to be above all the essence of its country: the landscape in a bottle.

Choosing Wine in Tuscany

The old and new worlds of wine cohabit in Tuscany as they do in few other places. The curious visitor will make sure to enjoy both to the full.

A sense of humour is almost as important as a corkscrew in the confusing world of Italian wine. Most of the confusion is caused by the uncontrollable enthusiasm of producers. While deep conservatism reigns at the small producer level, medium-sized players seem game for any experiment to raise their profile – and most of the best producers come into this category; estates as varied in size as, for example, the châteaux of Bordeaux.

"*Il genuino*" is a phrase you often hear among small farmers and innkeepers. It expresses their deep suspicion of anything that is not of their own making, by unsophisticated methods but often in complete innocence of background knowledge. Wine that is *genuino* may be halfway to vinegar, but to be *trafficato* – in their view – would be worse. ("Trafficking" could be anything from a very necessary application of sulphur, to using grapes or adding wine imported from the Mezzogiorno – a long-established practice all over northern Italy.)

Many genuinely believe, too, that simple peasant wine, for all its faults, leaves you with a clearer head.

No visitor should miss the opportunity of tasting rustic wine (*il genuino*) if only to learn how radical recent progress has been. Peasant white wines are generally yellow (*giallo*) with oxidation and flat in flavour, perhaps just sharpening with the onset of vinegar. They taste better unchilled, and demand food. The open carafe wine in simple fishermen's restaurants is usually in this tradition, and would instantly be poured down the sink by anyone with a new-world education in "wine faults". For those with a sense of history and a love of Europe, though, they are worth tasting, before moving on to something bottled and labelled (at many times the price).

Red carafe wines are more variable, with a better chance of being palatable, and a long-odds chance of being *à point*, full of fruit and life and bite. I make a point of tasting them, whether at simple roadside tables or where a sommelier has had a hand in the selection.

In tourist restaurants, lists of bottled wines have become interminable as the producers turn their hands to whatever strikes their fancy – and the sommelier tries to keep up. Thus in Chianti the wine list will probably include a score of the better-known makers (and generally most local ones), each one with one or two varietal would-be Supertuscans as well as a Chianti and one or two vintages of Chianti Riservas (which are only made in good or goodish years). If your taste is for "safe", high-coloured, dense-fruity, oak-flavoured wines the varietals should be your choice, a choice greatly complicated by the habit of putting any useful information in tiny type on a back-label.

The labels of DOC-regulated wines (Chianti Classico is DOCG, but the theology of adding "Garantita" to "Controllata" has no place in this book) are relatively plain sailing. The producer and the DOC are the principal features – though few producers can resist adding a brand name, a vineyard name or just a fantasy name whose significance (if any) is unclear.

Tuscany is one of the few places where the best advice when in doubt is to choose one of the biggest and most famous names, Antinori being the shining example. Even the least expensive wine from such a house is a good buy. Ruffino, Frescobaldi and Ricasoli are other well-distributed blue chips.

The text puts a number of Tuscany's best producers in their local contexts. This page lists some of the terms to look for. Pages 139–142 list some wines that could be called benchmarks or that I particularly like. The list is far from being comprehensive – even of the latter. The most up-to-date and in-depth review of Italian wines is the annual *Gambero Rosso Guide*, published by Slow Food Editore and translated into English as *Italian Wines*.

DOC Denominazione d'Origine Controllata

The basic appellation system of Italy, started in 1963 and still growing as new wine-types are created. All wines (but not brands) anyone has ever heard of are "controlled" – up to a point – by the system. Theoretically there are well over one thousand.

DOCG

The same as DOC, but "guaranteed" by the law. The upper crust of appellations are now DOCG – including Chianti Classico. Exactly how the Italian government guarantees anything is not clear, but a numbered neck-label indicates at least quantity control.

IGT Indicazione Geografica Tipica

A recent appellation designed to prevent top wines made outside DOC regulation from falling into the default bracket of Vino da Tavola. IGT wines are often originals waiting to be sanctified as DOC (though nothing is guaranteed).

VDT Vino da Tavola

The humblest of appellations because it involves no controls – the very reason so many of the most imaginative wine-makers prefer it to DOC.

Riserva

Each DOC has a precise definition of how long a Riserva must be aged by the producer (in barrel and/or in bottle) before it can be so labelled. Riservas are the selected wines of better years that merit such aging, and offer more in character, intensity and complexity. *Annata* simply means the vintage year, Riserva or not.

Cantina

The *cantina* is a place where wine is made (press- or vat-house), the cellar where it is stored, or even a place where it is drunk.

Consorzio

A *consorzio* is a group of producers united in the defence and promotion of their DOC. The first was the "Gallo Nero", whose black cock appears on the neck-label of most Chianti Classicos. Note, though, that a small handful of the best producers have their own reasons for not belonging to the *consorzio*.

Fattoria

Fattoria is the most commonly used word for a wine farm (or indeed any farm). Theoretically it is distinct in that it is run by what the Scottish call a factor, or estate manager (*fattore*). A grander estate is sometimes called a *tenuta*, and a more humble one a *podere*. A *castello* is simply a *fattoria* with a castle.

A Selection of Wines from Each Tuscan Region

THE ARNO VALLEY: FLORENCE TO THE SEA

RUFINA

The Frescobaldi estates of Nipozzano and Pomino dominate the region. Montesodi is their top Rufina Chianti. Fattoria Selvapiana and Basciano are the other upholders of the Rufina district and its splendid wines.

This is also the place to mention the wines of the big firm of Ruffino, based at Pontassieve. Their Chianti Classico Riserva Ducale is noble, and Cabreo Il Borgo introduces Cabernet to make a wine comparable to Carmignano.

CARMIGNANO

Wines from Villa Capezzana are the standard-setters, and not expensive. All are good: Vin Ruspo a lively rosé, Barco Reale lightish fruity red, Capezzana Riservas built for long life. Ghiaie della Furba is their Supertuscan Cabernet blend. Fattoria Ambra and the Medici Villa Artimino (which has a useful hotel next door) are

other producers. Chiantis from here are called Chianti Montalbano and are often worth trying.

LUCCA AND NEARBY

Montecarlo wines from Buonamico, Montechiari and the Fattoria del Teso. But be adventurous with the whites from the Colline Lucchesi, whether the name is familiar or not.

SOUTH OF FLORENCE: CHIANTI COUNTRY

CHIANTI COLLI FIORENTINI

Castello di Poppiano at Montespertoli, Castello del Trebbio at Santa Brigida, Fattoria La Querce at Impruneta.

CHIANTI CLASSICO

The list of good producers is long, and few will agree who is best. The following, grouped by district, can make wonderful wines – both classic Chiantis and Super-

tuscan-type blends. They are listed here by communes to give an idea of their distribution – though to say that this indicates their style is a bold assertion. All that can generally be said is that the further south in the Classico zone you go, the more full-bodied the wines are likely to be.

At Barberino Val d'Elsa (to the west) Casa Emma, Isole e Olena (also top Cabernet, Syrah and Vin Santo), Castello di Monsanto, Pasolini Dall'Onda.

At Castellina in Chianti (central) Tenuta de Bibbiano, Castellare, Villa Cerna, Castello de Fonterutoli (also Siepi, excellent Sangiovese/Merlot), Brancaia, Lilliano, Rocca delle Macie, San Fabiano Calcinaia.

At Castelnuovo Berardenga (south) Fattoria di Felsina is rightly renowned; San Felice makes many good wines.

At San Casciano in Val di Pesa (northwest) The headquarters of the house of

Antinori. The top wines are the famous Solaia and Tignanello, but the Chiantis, Marchese Antinori, Badia a Passignano and the fruity Peppoli are models, too. Also Fattoria di Grevepesa, Le Corti-Corsini and the Fattoria Macchiavelli-Serristori.

At Gaiole in Chianti (south central) Chianti Geografico is the admirable growers' cooperative. Castello di Ama is outstanding for a range of varietals as well as its top Chianti Classico Bellavista. Badia a Coltibuono is a beautiful ex-monastery in the hills with a restaurant and many old vintages. The Castello di Brolio is the *locus classicus* of Chianti: the Ricasoli wines are now impeccable (after a bad patch). Riecine is an English favourite; Cacchiano and Lamole di Lamole are both famous old names.

At Greve in Chianti (north central) Carpineto, Nozzole (Ruffino property), Querceto and Querciabella are all excellent – especially the latter (*quercia* means oaktree). The castles of Uzzano, Verrazzano and Vicchiomaggio are all landmarks. Vignamaggio supplied the first Chianti ever recorded.

At Panzano in Chianti (central) Tenuta Fontodi is the outstanding producer – also of good Syrah. Cennatoio, Castello dei Rampolla, Villa Cafaggio and Vecchie Terre di Montefili are reliable or better.

At Poggibonsi (to the west) Melini is one of the region's best-known brands. Their top wine is La Selvanella. They also make Vernaccia di San Gimignano.

At Radda in Chianti (southeast) Castello di Albola, Volpaia and Montevertine are all in the top league, the latter famous for Sangiovese Le Pergole Torte. Note also Fattoria Terrabianca.

At Tavarnelle Val di Pesa (west) Poggio al Sole is to be recommended (also for red varietals).

At San Gimignano Vernaccias (and red wines) from Guicciardini-Strozzi's Fattoria di Cusona, Fattoria Paradiso and Ponte a Rondolino's Terre di Tufi are prestigious. Other good wines come from Baroncini, Falchini, La Lastra, Montenidoli, Mormoraia, Panizzi, Fattoria San Donato, Teruzzi e Puthod and Fratelli Vagnoni at Pancole.

SIENA AND THE SOUTH

MONTALCINO
Visit the *enoteca* in the *fortezza* to get an idea of the number of producers (and the alarming prices some charge).

Biondi-Santi stands out as the original. Then, in no particular order: Altesino; Argiano; the mammoth Castello Banfi with many wines; Fattoria dei Barbi; Caparzo (La Casa is best); the Frescobaldi family's Castelgiocondo, with excellent Merlot Lamaione, and their Mondavi joint-ventures, Luce and Lucente; Col d'Orcia (with a lovely tasting room); Costanti; Il Poggione; Lisini (on the dirt road east from Sant'Angelo in Colle); Mastrojanni; Nardi; Angelo Gaja's Pieve Santa Restituta; Poggio Antico; Marroneto; Castello Romitorio; and Val di Suga. Do not forget to try the Rosso di Montalcino wherever you see it.

MONTEPULCIANO

Avignonesi and Poliziano are the top names in Montepulciano, for varietals as well as Vino Nobile, and Avignonesi's amazing Vin Santo. Boscarelli, Canneto, Fattoria del Cerro, Contucci, Fanetti, Fassati, Innocenti, Il Macchione, Antinori's La Braccesca, Ruffino's Lodola Nuova, Tenuta Trerose and Tenuta Valdipiatta are all ambitious to restore the fame of Vino Nobile. Montepulciano is also, however, included in the zone of Chianti Colli Senesi, the Chianti of Siena, so many local producers make a Chianti, too. And some also make a pleasant mild white called Bianco Vergine di Valdichiana,

though this is losing ground to the more fashionable Chardonnay, Sauvignon Blanc and the rest.

THE VAL D'ORCIA

In this valley south of Montepulciano, Tenuta di Trinoro (for massive Bordeaux-style reds).

THE TUSCAN COAST

THE PROVINCE OF PISA

The new world of Tuscan coastal wines has a remote outpost between Livorno and Bolgheri, with the DOCs of Montescudaio Val di Cornia. The Tenuta del Terriccio at Castellino Marittima makes an excellent Cabernet/Merlot called Lupicaia, and a Chardonnay/Sauvignon Blanc called Fondinaia, both of which are high in the Supertuscan league.

BOLGHERI

Bolgheri rosato is the affordable wine in this millionaire enclave. Mortgages are needed for the wonderful Paleo, Grattamacco, Sassicaia (Cabernet), Masseto (Merlot) and Guado al Tasso and Ornellaia (both Cabernet/Merlot). Poggio alle Gazze is excellent Sauvignon Blanc, but the hot tip for value and character is the white Vermentino from Antinori's Tenuta Belvedere.

South of Bolgheri, near the coast at Suvereto, the estates of Tua Rita, Monte-peloso and Gualdo del Re are in the DOC Val di Cornia, making fashionably modern wines. Note the Vermentino here, too.

THE ISLAND OF ELBA

Acquabona at Portoferraio, La Chiusa at Magazzini, Enrico Tirloni at Lacona – but try any island wine.

THE SOUTHERN MAREMMA

Standards here are rising rapidly. Possibly the most delicious Morellino of the moment is Mazzei's Tenuta di Belguardo, from near Montiano. Then the best producers of Morellino di Scansano are Le Pupille at Pereta, Moris Farms at Massa Marittima, Erik Banti and Bargagli's Provveditore at Scansano, and the original Mantellasi at Magliano. La Parrina is a big coastal estate near Porto Santo Stefano, with its own DOC for not very special red and white (but good cheese in the dairy).

BIANCO DI PITIGLIANO DOC

These are very light but fresh whites. La Stellata near Manciano makes very drinkable Lunaia. Bargagli at Scansano and Sassotondo at Sovana are alternatives, and others are offered to visitors in the cellars of the ancient gateway of Pitigliano. Look out for Antinori's future productions in the district.

A Selection of Grape Varieties

Aleatico A red, muscat-scented grape grown mainly on Elba. Well worth trying.

Ansonica You may have to go to the little island of Giglio (ferry from Porto Santo Stefano) to drink this better-than-Trebbiano white with excellent fish.

Brunello Montalcino's form of the universal red Sangiovese, a clone that in the relatively warm conditions of the region makes Tuscany's biggest and boldest wines.

Cabernet Sauvignon Now common in Tuscany as the ideal blending partner to Sangiovese (though in the colder parts of Chianti Merlot ripens better). Has found its perfect home on the coast at Bolgheri.

Canaiolo One of the increasingly rare black grapes used in the Chianti blend, particularly for the traditional *governo*.

Colorino Another, with usefully dark colour. Now not often found.

Malvasia One of Tuscany's two best white grapes, though mainly used for blending in Chianti. On its own prone to oxidation if not handled with care. Can age to rich, gentle, almost voluptuous dry wine.

Mammolo Another traditional red companion of Sangiovese, dark and pungent, but now uncommon.

Merlot Recently popular as a Sangiovese partner and very good on its own, both inland and on the coast.

Moscadello Montalcino once had its own muscat variety, known as Moscadelleto, for strong, sweet, amber wines that lived for decades. Its modern muscats of Moscadello are more in the light Asti vein.

Procanico An archaic synonym for Trebbiano.

Prugnolo Gentile The dominant form (or clone) of Sangiovese in Montepulciano.

Sangiovese Tuscany's major red grape, with many clones, the best of which are Sangiovese Grosso (with bigger grapes) and include Brunello and Prugnolo Gentile. Chianti is essentially a Sangiovese blend, but as the grape is better understood and cultivated it will be seen more often as a straight varietal.

Trebbiano The far-too-common workhorse white grape of Tuscany, and much of Italy, a big producer of sharp, tasteless wine. Some is labelled as Galestro after the shaly soil that seemingly gives the best. Its French names are Ugni Blanc and St Emilion – the necessarily sharp (and prolific) distilling wine for Cognac.

Vermentino A similar white grape to Malvasia, excellent in Corsica and Sardinia and on the coast of Liguria (just north of Tuscany) and beginning to make its mark as the new Tuscan white. It should be soft-textured and full-flavoured, dry and appetizing.

Vernaccia di San Gimignano A potentially full-bodied, tasty and original white, though for years made almost as tasteless as Trebbiano. Worth tasting around.

ACKNOWLEDGMENTS

Hugh Johnson's Acknowledgments

I have discovered Tuscany and its wines gradually over the past 35 years, through the kindness of many people. Recently and especially including Burton Anderson, Piero Antinori, Arcigola Slow Food, Ugo Contini Bonacossi, Duncan Baird, Leonardo Frescobaldi, Tiziana Frescobaldi, Gelasio Gaetani d'Aragona Lovatelli, Brian and Diana Johnson, Andreas März, Filippo Mazzei, Franceso Ricasoli, Giacomo Tachis, Peter Vinding-Diers.

Commissioned Photographs

Andy Katz:
Pages 1, 2, 4–5, 7, 8, 16, 23, 30–31, 32, 37, 38, 40, 41, 45, 46, 47, 48, 49, 50–51, 55, 59, 60, 61, 67, 72, 79, 85, 86, 90, 93, 94, 97, 102, 104, 105, 108, 110, 112, 113, 114–115, 117, 135, 144

Max Alexander:
Pages 15, 19, 42, 43, 44, 52, 56, 57, 58, 62, 63, 64, 69, 70, 71, 74, 75, 76, 77, 80, 81, 82, 83, 84, 89, 92, 96, 98, 99, 100–101, 103, 107, 118, 121, 122, 123, 126, 128, 130, 131, 132–133, 136, 138, 140–141

Other Photographs
The publishers would like to thank the following photographers, agencies and copyright holders for their kind permission to reproduce the following photographs in this book:

Archivo Fratelli Alinari, Florence:
Pages 12, 24, 27

Eduardo Fornaciari:
Page 28

Enoteca Pinchiorri, Florence/Paolo Cecconi:
Page 34

The Stockmarket, London:
Pages 35, 36

John Ferro Sims, London:
Pages 68, 79, 109, 124, 125

Ken Adlard:
Endpapers

The endpapers are taken from the map Toscana published by Touring Club Italiano, Milan, and reproduced with their kind permission.